MADDIE AND US

The Story Of A Lost Musical

Shaun McKenna

ISBN 9798645610098

For Jenny

for coming to love the other woman
as much as I do.

No musical reaches the West End without the creative input, love and support of a host of people. The writing team would like to thank everybody who has given their time, commitment and dedication to Maddie in its various incarnations.

In writing this book, I would particularly like to thank the major contributors - Steven Dexter, Stephen Keeling, Kenny Wax, Caroline Humphris, Niki Turner, Jonathan Church, Lee Menzies, Martin Lowe, Graham Bickley, Barry Brown, Kevin Colson and Summer Rognlie.

Debts of gratitude are also due to my late wife, Jenny, for her support over the eight years of the project; and to Rachel Daniels, my agent, who (as you will see) managed to wade through many complex and muddy contractual difficulties.

CONTENTS

ABOUT THIS BOOK

The first ten chapters of this book were written in 1997 and completed the week before *Maddie* opened at the Lyric Theatre, Shaftesbury Avenue. Hopes were high. James Hogan at Oberon Books had commissioned this book to tell the story of the show we were sure would be a hit.

It wasn't. Though there were some great reviews, there were an equal number of absolute stinkers. It was a first West End show for all of us and a bruising experience to open a newspaper and read that our much-loved offspring, to whom we had devoted years of our lives, was malformed, hideous and deserved to be killed as quickly as possible. It takes a bit of experience to learn that you can't pay any attention to reviews. Great shows I've been involved with have been savaged in the press and frankly poor shows lauded to the skies.

The hurt passes. Attitudes change. You discover that reviews are really only marketing tools, useful if there's something you can put on the poster, in press ads or, these days, on the net.

Apart from an abortive flurry of activity around 2009 (described in Chapter 11), none of us had thought much about *Maddie* until Tim Hutton of Stage Door Records approached us at the beginning of 2016 with a plan to reissue the original London cast album. He had in mind a twentieth anniversary celebration of a 'lost' musical.

Tim was keen to add a second CD of many of the demo recordings of songs that had been cut or radically changed in the show's eight year development. We all had some reservations about the version we played at the Lyric in 1997 and wanted to reinstate some of the cut numbers – even to add new ones here and there. It seemed an excellent opportunity to have versions of all the *Maddie* songs in one place.

Tim's love, care and attention to detail turned the CD re-release into more than that. It reignited our passion for the show.

At a meeting in Summer 2016 I mentioned the existence of this book. Tim asked to read it and then began his second campaign – to persuade us to publish it. Tim thought a story about what it was like to be unknown writers getting a show on in the 1990s would be of interest. After all, some of the great names of the era wander through these pages.

James at Oberon did not feel that enough readers would be prepared to buy a book about a forgotten flop (my description, not his). Tim felt differently and has put an enormous amount of work into getting what follows in front of you. There was another three year delay before we finally did it – but as you will discover, in *Maddie* terms, three years is nothing.

And Keeling, Dexter and I? Well, it feels as though we've been re-introduced to an old friend. When *Maddie* flopped we all thought it was the end, but it wasn't. We have all gone on to enjoy careers with pretty much the usual proportion of triumphs and disasters. I can't help having a sneaky feeling that the show, like its heroine, is somehow refusing to die – at least, not until she has shown the world she really did have what it takes.

So, to practical matters.

The first ten chapters are exactly as written in 1997. Amendments or comments in hindsight are made in square brackets and italics. Everything from Chapter 11 onwards is new. Everyone quoted directly in the original book has given their permission to be quoted in this one.

Enjoy.

Shaun McKenna
April 2020

FOREWORD

by Sir Cameron Mackintosh

I've always had a sneaking regard for Sitting Bull's advice to Annie Oakley in *Annie Get Your Gun*. 'Don't put your money in Showbusiness.' It's one of the riskiest businesses on earth and yet for many one of the most attractive. The musical theatre, of all the live branches of the Arts, is the most risky and difficult to pull off and yet I don't think it is a coincidence that many of the most successful musicals, including the 'first' one, *Showboat,* were usually considered hopeless projects by people who 'knew' before they opened. *Oklahoma!* opened as *Away We Go* to a chorus of, 'No Gals, No Gags, No Chance' out of town, and *Les Miserables* opened to a Glum reception in London.

The fact is that the theatre survives and is constantly reinvigorated by one thing alone and that is original new writing which captures the public imagination. No open cheque book can buy a real success and no lavish scenery can save a dumb story. Sure, a smart producer is an asset but even then there is no secret recipe lodged in a bank vault. The great British producer, Charles B. Cochrane, always gave aspiring producers the same sage advice, 'Never put on a show for the public: put it on for yourself because you love it, do it as well as you can and then, hopefully, the public will come and share your enthusiasm.' I've always felt that a producer needs common sense, persistence, flair and, as Alfred P. Doolittle so admirably put it, 'a little bit of luck.' But, of course, first of all he needs to find the material to nurture.

When I was asked to set up a Chair for a visiting professor at Oxford University, I knew I would only do it if it was a Chair that encompassed both contemporary drama and contemporary musical theatre. Happily the University concurred and we unanimously agreed that we could have no better inaugural professor than the legendary Stephen Sondheim, whose work always encompassed both music and drama. Stephen's hugely successful year was marked by a series of Masterclasses in the writing of musicals. The University sent out an open invitation for writers to take part and Stephen (aided slightly by me) chose a dozen writers, mostly in sets of composer and lyricist, to work with him on various projects. He purposely chose the widest range of styles and made everyone work together so that they were able to observe each other's different working methods and also understand how to respect the very different styles of shows their colleagues were writing. They all had the same professional aim - to write a successful musical. The projects ranged from *Yusupov*, about Rasputin and the Russian Tzars, to *Eyam*, a story of the plague. But there was one project that just wanted to be a musical comedy and not a serious musical play. That was *Maddie*, a musical by Stephen Keeling, Shaun McKenna and Steven Dexter, based on a movie called *Maxie*. At the end of the year, Stephen staged excerpts from each production and in the showcase *Maddie* strutted her enjoyable stuff. One member of the audience was an ambitious young producer, Kenneth Wax, whom I had met when he first started in the business and had worked as an intern on one of my productions. Even then I knew Kenny was well on his way to gathering all the necessary ingredients to become a successful producer. He was born with charm and persistence so the other qualities were only a matter of time. He took up the project and after a tremendous amount of work got together a fully-fledged tryout production at Salisbury Playhouse where the show received very encouraging notices. But he knew it still needed work and he made sure it got it before he finally made the plunge to bring it to the West End eight years after the show was written. *West Side Story* took nearly ten years, starting out as *East Side Story*, and then Leonard Bernstein stopped writing and wrote *Candide* in between. *Guys And Dolls* started as a serious musical like *South Pacific* and went through twelve librettists before it became a classic. *Pygmalion* was considered too difficult by every leading writer of musicals including Lerner and Loewe before it became *My Fair Lady* several years later on. Only time will tell if *Maddie* is a goodie but it won't be for want of care, love and professionalism if it isn't. Its creators are all madly in love with the musical theatre and that's what counts in the end.

INTRODUCTION

In those old MGM movies, a team of young hopefuls (usually Judy Garland and Mickey Rooney) put on a show in their own back yard because nobody else will give them a chance. There are apparently insuperable difficulties, heartbreak and impending disaster but somehow they get the show on in time. A big producer just happens to be in the audience, leading to fame, fortune and happy endings for all concerned.

It was never like that!

Or was it? It all depends how you tell the story. The saga of how *Maddie* finally came to the stage of the Lyric Theatre, Shaftesbury Avenue contains enough amazing strokes of luck, fortunate coincidences and the intervention of big showbusiness names (not to mention trials and tribulations, lies, deceit, death and desperation) to furnish half a dozen old movies. It took, however, a lot more than ninety minutes to reach a happy ending.

Stephen Keeling, Steven Dexter and Shaun McKenna, the writers of *Maddie,* have often said that the story for their second musical should be how they finally managed to get their first show produced. The trouble is, nobody would believe it - and it would take too long to tell. It would also have a cast of thousands.

This is that story. It is told largely in chronological order and the focus changes with every chapter. Writers and composers will find the nuts and bolts of how the music, book and lyrics evolved and how an unwieldy story was honed for the musical stage; aspiring producers will find lessons in the actions of Kenneth Wax, who finally got the show to the West End, and other producers who didn't; there are sections on raising investment, on casting, on directing and orchestrating and on designing, as well as the experiences of performers and theatre technicians. The story covers eight years, from the formation of the writing team to critical and audience responses to the West End production. The story of Maddie may continue to encompass further success in the UK and elsewhere, or it may end in premature closure and the loss of a great deal of money. Either way it is a story which has a great deal to say about the state of the modern theatre world - and musical theatre in particular.

OVERTURE AND BEGINNERS

While all theatre is a collaborative exercise, a musical is the *most* collaborative form of theatre yet invented. Whereas in a straight play the basic elements of the creative team might consist of a producer, writer, director, designer, lighting designer and sound designer, for a musical you must add, at the very least, composer, lyricist, musical director, orchestrator and choreographer to the mix. The process begins with the writing team - and even then, in forging a working relationship, they bring their own motivations, prejudices and ambitions to bear, along with their talent.

Maddie is a musical comedy about a girl who comes back from the dead to complete unfinished business. Her return to life is brought about by the combination of many forces, both physical and supernatural. Sometimes it has seemed as though those same forces were working together to bring *Maddie*, the show, into being.

In 1989, Steven Dexter was 27. He was born Stephen Errol Davids in Cape Town on August 26th 1962. He and his English parents emigrated to Israel in 1974 and lived on Kibbutz Mishmar David. When Dexter applied for an Israeli passport, 'Stephen' was spelled 'Steven' - and 'Steven' is what he became. Steven Davids did his compulsory Israeli National Service from 1980-83 and subsequently travelled to Britain, where in 1984 he began the two year Stage Management and Technical Theatre course at LAMDA (The London Academy of Music and Dramatic Art). He went directly to the stage management team of the Croydon Warehouse Theatre. When applying for Equity membership, he found he was unable to use his own name (Equity rules forbid the duplication of names - hence so many stage names.) He wanted to keep his own initials. Finding his first choice, Steven Daniels, was also already taken he went through the telephone book and came up with 'Dexter.'

He had loved musicals from a very early age. Because his parents were English, he made many trips to the UK during his childhood and teens and had caught up with all the big musicals playing in London. His ambition had always been to direct them.

In the summer of 1989, Dexter was working on *Budgie* at the Cambridge Theatre, a new musical starring Adam Faith, based on his 1970s hit TV series. As part of the stage management team, Dexter had an opportunity to watch at close quarters how a new musical was put together. With the *Budgie* company surrounding him, he was looking into the possibility of mounting and directing a one-night charity performance - but didn't know what the show should be.

At the same time, to earn extra money, he worked at Dress Circle, the specialist musical theatre shop in Covent Garden's Monmouth Street. Dress Circle's huge stock of recordings, libretti and material about virtually every musical ever written allowed him to rapidly (and enjoyably) expand his knowledge of the musical theatre heritage, as well as keeping him up to date with all the new shows in the UK and America. He knew he wanted to find something extra special to direct as his first show.
Budgie closed before Dexter found the right piece for his planned one-nighter. He moved on to the stage management team of *M. Butterfly*, starring Anthony Hopkins, at the Shaftesbury Theatre. He was still actively looking for a project.

Dexter's family was a key influence. At the end of one of her visits to London, his sister Maureen said, 'I wish I'd seen a musical.' Dexter, having spent a small fortune on tickets to ten top West End shows, asked her what she meant. She said, 'I mean a proper musical. Something that makes me feel good, that sends me out humming the tunes and wanting to dance down the street.' She felt that she had not seen a show with a positive message, that said something about life and the importance of living it to the full. This gave Dexter something else to think about when planning his charity one-nighter.

Dexter's mother, Myra Davids, had always told her son, 'Stop thinking about tomorrow and what might happen. You could be dead tomorrow. Live for today.' In the summer of 1989 Myra passed away. As Dexter watched his mother dying he thought, 'You're right. Enough of saying I want to be a director. I'm going to do something about it.'

Influenced by his mother's death, Dexter's mind turned to spiritual matters and the eternal question, 'What happens when we die?' There had never been a successful musical about a ghost - and it was a subject that fascinated him. It also provided plenty of interesting visual opportunities for phantoms, floating chairs, ectoplasm and all the other supernatural paraphenalia. He looked at several ideas. Noel Coward's *Blithe Spirit* had already been adapted as *High Spirits*, so he flirted for a while with John van Druten's charming witchcraft fable, *Bell, Book and Candle* - which had provided the basis of the fondly-remembered, long-running American TV series, *Bewitched.* For Dexter, though, the idea did not quite click.

He had a flat in Shadwell, East London, and had recently installed cable television. One night, after two performances of *M. Butterfly*, he got a phone call from his friend Peter Bull *[who would subsequently go on to found London's first dedicated LGBT theatre, Above The Stag, first in Victoria and subsequently in Vauxhall]* telling him to turn on the TV. A film was playing that might fit the bill. Dexter turned it on, ran a bath and went for a long soak in it, leaving the TV playing in the living room. Gradually, the soundtrack attracted his attention - it was a film about a woman being possessed by the spirit of a long-dead wannabe film star. He became intrigued, jumped out of the bath, and watched the final half hour. The film was *Maxie*, starring Glenn Close, Mandy Patinkin and Ruth Gordon.

Fortunately, cable TV stations repeat films three or four times and Dexter set his video to record the whole of *Maxie* at its next showing. He watched it several times and fell in love with the idea and spirit of the piece - someone coming back from the dead to have another chance. He lived with the story for a few weeks, mulling it over in his head while travelling back and forth to work, and during performances at the Shaftesbury. He broke down the plot to its key elements and tried to work out how to reconstruct it in musical comedy form. It seemed quite straightforward.

Dexter did not have an agent at the time. He was working as an assistant stage manager on a West End show and was a member of Equity - that was the extent of his connections. He had no hands on experience of creating a show from scratch but he decided to trust his instinct that *Maxie* would 'sing.' He set about getting a team together.

In early July 1989, he had seen a workshop production of *The Devil and Mr Stone* at the Donmar Warehouse. *Mr Stone* was based on the age-old Faust legend. This was the second musical by twenty three year-old Stephen Keeling.

Keeling hailed from rural North Staffordshire, where he was born in 1966. When he was about eleven, his school presented a musical production of a novel called *The Black Cauldron* (a book which Disney would later film). The school show was scripted and composed by the music teacher, Robin Moody. Keeling played the leading role, Taran the pig boy, and he was tremendously excited and impressed by the power of the musical form. He learned the songs by heart (and can still play them). After that, he began to write little plays with music - both based on fairytales and some original tales of his own. He did not listen to musicals - they were simply not part of his environment.

His next major influence was the local vicar's wife, Anthea Deakin. She had been to RADA and would have loved to have been an actress - she also had a talent for writing. Mrs Deakin and Keeling proved to be kindred spirits. Before long, the vicar's wife and the teenage boy decided to write shows together. They formed a drama group, The Hobbits, for children in the area, and put on the shows they were writing (There was also an adult group, the Bumpkins, but they refused to have anything to do with the work of the precocious youngster). Keeling and Deakin worked on many shows up to, and after, the time he went to Goldsmith's College to study music. Shows he particularly remembers are their version of *Scrooge* and - when he was at Goldsmith's - the show he still considers his first real musical - *Creation Story*, a *Jesus Christ Superstar*-influenced version of the book of Genesis, which was performed at the National Garden Festival in Stoke on Trent.

Keeling's favourite theatre composers, and greatest influences, were George Gershwin and Leonard Bernstein - both their songs and longer orchestral works.

One of the cast of *Creation Story* sent the score to the composer Stephen Oliver, who had written, with Tim Rice, the musical *Blondel* as well as the music for the RSC's *Nicholas Nickleby* and Radio Four's dramatisation of Tolkien's *Lord of the Rings.* Oliver encouraged the young composer, going through *Creation Story* with him note by note, and commenting that the music was very four-square - everything was in balanced phrases of four. For a while after that, everything Keeling wrote was in phrases or three or five, with nothing matching exactly.
The musical influences at Goldsmith's were heavily weighted in favour of twentieth century atonal music - the antithesis of Keeling's natural and developing style. This was particularly true of his composition teacher, with whom he had some profound disagreements. In fact, after one contretemps, Keeling was sacked from the composition course. Keeling told nobody about his musical theatre work or his ambitions to write musicals - which the Goldsmith's people would have considered trivial, even though Keeling was musical director on a Goldsmith's production of *Superstar*.

On graduating, Keeling worked professionally as a musical director, spending a lengthy period at the Library Theatre in Manchester. He was still not familiar with many musical scores other than the work of Lloyd Webber - and Barbra Streisand's *Broadway* album, where he first heard songs by Stephen Sondheim. It was at the Manchester Library that Keeling's knowledge of both contemporary and classic musicals grew. The theatre had presented the UK premieres of both *Follies* and *Pacific Overtures* and was steeped in Sondheim. Stephen worked his way through all the Sondheim shows and particularly admired the musical theatre writing of Leonard Bernstein. It was here, too, that he came to know and admire the big Broadway sound of Jule Styne and Jerry Herman.

Creation Story had led to a friendship between Keeling and Dennis Pickford, a poet, who played God in the Stoke-on-Trent production. Keeling went to Pickford with the idea for *The Devil and Mr Stone* and they worked on it for two years, finally hiring the Donmar Warehouse to present a three-night showcase in the summer of 1989. The Donmar was being renovated at the time. When they arrived for the second performance, they discovered that the builders had been in - their set (which largely consisted of tables and chairs) was covered in lumps of dried concrete. All they could do was to cover all the furniture with sheets of plastic.

Dexter was impressed and intrigued by the young, blond composer ('He looked about twelve,' says Dexter) who was so passionate about his music. While Dexter felt that *Mr Stone* was flawed, particularly in terms of book and lyrics, the score was very strong. It was interesting, evocative, full of surprises and emotional. Most importantly, it had a distinctive voice, which Dexter found very exciting. Finding an unknown composer whose work did not sound like that of a dozen other composers was a surprisingly rare event.

Dexter was still working at Dress Circle to supplement his income. One afternoon, Keeling came into the shop. Dexter recognised him immediately from the Donmar show and said something along the lines of, 'Hello, I'm Steven Dexter. I was very impressed with your show. Do you want to write a musical together?'

Keeling was intrigued, not least by the directness of the approach. Dexter lent him the videotape of *Maxie,* which Keeling took home and watched. As Dexter had been, he was immediately attracted by the film's premise. He felt that it was crying out to be a big, Broadway-style musical. He was also curious to see whether he could write a score in that genre, which was totally unlike his usual style. *Creation Story* had been a rock opera, *The Devil And Mr Stone* in the style of *Les Miserables.* Like Dexter, Keeling loved the Jule Styne sound of shows like *Funny Girl* and decided that he was attracted to the challenge.

A week or so later, Dexter and Keeling met up outside the Shaftesbury Theatre and went for tea in Di's Diner. They talked through the potential of the movie and, over a pot of Earl Grey, became a team. The next step was to find the right lyricist. Though Dexter knew he wanted to be involved in creating the book of the show, he did not have the confidence to take it entirely upon himself, and felt he needed a collaborator.

Through *Budgie*, he vaguely knew Don Black, the distinguished lyricist who would go on to add *Sunset Boulevard* and *The Goodbye Girl* to his impressive list of credits. Dexter took the project to him but he declined, saying that he thought a book musical stood little chance of popular success in the prevailing climate. Neither Dexter nor Keeling knew another lyricist whom they thought would capture the necessary feel - and were not in a position to approach the established names. So they placed an advertisement in *The Stage.* In retrospect, that seems like a naive way of proceeding - ads in *The Stage* normally attract responses from the less-successful echelons of showbusiness. However, the ad duly appeared for a 'lyricist to work with composer Stephen Keeling on a new musical project. Witty, bright style required. Send examples of work to...'

While they were waiting for the ad to appear, Keeling and Dexter talked at length about capturing the contrasting sounds of the show - the 1920s flapper world of Maxie Malone and the contemporary world of Nick and Jan Cheyney. Keeling went away and wrote some tunes, returning a week later to play the song which would eventually become *The Time of My Life*, a nostalgic, reflective ballad. Dexter adored it immediately. It remains the oldest song in the show, surviving umpteen rewrites. Keeling also wrote a patter song for two comic priests (characters who did not even make it to the first draft) and a party song, during which Maxie Malone makes an exhibition of herself.

Pink Hippo Productions Ltd
are looking for a
LYRICIST
to work with the composer Stephen Keeling on a new musical project. Witty, bright style required.
Send examples of work to:
Pink Hippo Prod's Ltd, 139 The Ryde, Hatfield, Herts AL9 5DP

One of the people who saw the *Stage* ad was Shaun McKenna, a 32-year old writer living in Brighton. McKenna was a former actor who had taken to teaching drama as a means of making a living and was now struggling to establish himself as a playwright. He had had a couple of professional writing jobs and had recently obtained his first big commission, to adapt Richard Llewellyn's *How Green Was My Valley* for the Royal Theatre, Northampton. McKenna was working as a commercial producer for Brighton's local radio station, Southern Sound. He was at least fulfilling one of his ambitions - to make his living by writing - even if writing thirty second commercials for local pine warehouses was not exactly what he had had in mind.

McKenna had been a musical nut from the age of eight, when he first saw a double bill of *The Wizard of Oz* and *Tom Thumb* at the local ABC cinema. It was a taste he shared with his wife, Jenny - they often spent Sunday afternoons watching re-runs of the classic films. He was a devotee of the big, robust, in-your-face Rodgers and Hammerstein shows like *Carousel* and *South Pacific*, which were not afraid to pin their hearts on their sleeves. He particularly admired the Styne-Sondheim *Gypsy*, along with *West Side Story* and Kander and Ebb's *Chicago*. All three had brilliant Books as well as memorable songs. McKenna also admired the brilliant, witty shows of Stephen Sondheim which had taken musical theatre in a new direction. He had been introduced to these when he took the cast album of *Side By Side By Sondheim* out of Balham Record Library and did not return it for nearly two months.

McKenna's step-daughter, Deborah Gibbs, was working on the stage management team of the out-of-town tryout of Steven Schwartz's *The Baker's Wife* at the Wolsey Theatre in Ipswich. The weekend before Dexter and Keeling's *Stage* ad appeared, McKenna had seen the Ipswich show and, driving home down the M11, had said, 'I'd like to write a musical. Pity I don't know any decent composers.'

McKenna answered the ad. He was a little cautious and suspicious but thought he had nothing to lose by trying it on a 'suck it and see' basis. The problem was that he did not have any sample material to send. So he spent the next week writing four (fortunately now lost!) sample lyrics and, when it came to the accompanying letter, simply lied:

> As you will see from the enclosed CV I am primarily a playwright... However, back in 1985 I was involved in the production of an updated version of *Cinderella* for which I provided the lyrics - I enclose a few examples. Opportunities for writing lyrics have not come my way since- a pity, since it was an area of theatre writing that I enjoyed...

He posted the letter and settled down to wait for a response. He waited quite a while.

Keeling and Dexter were inundated with nearly two hundred applications. There were lyrics of hugely varying quality - it took a long time to sift the two-foot high pile of submissions and whittle the contenders down to a short list. Interestingly, that pile contained work by some lyricists who have gone on to make a mark in the theatre - including a few whose work Dexter has subsequently directed.

After a couple of months, McKenna and three others were invited to an interview. These took place, one Sunday in October, in a West End café. McKenna was extremely nervous, thinking he was going to meet a team of high-powered producers. He and his wife had been away for the weekend and he sent her off to traipse round Covent Garden in the pouring rain because 'it would look unprofessional' if she turned up with him at the café. She got drenched.

McKenna was the last of the four short-listed lyricists to be interviewed. While he was waiting, he managed to overhear some of the things that Dexter and Keeling were telling his predecessor, so he was well-prepared when his turn came. His eavesdropping enabled him to give the impression of being immediately in tune with the project. Dexter outlined the story of the film, *Maxie*, and Keeling had prepared a tape of the three songs from the show. Each of the short-listed lyricists were asked to go away and set them. It was effectively an audition.

Driving home to Brighton that evening, McKenna waited until he was on the M23 before slipping the tape into the car stereo. When the first strains of *The Time of My Life* came through the speakers, he was hooked. It was immediately catchy, romantic and nostalgic. It genuinely felt like a song from a classic show. The comic patter song, too, had a bubbling sense of fun. The party song was brassy and ballsy, though musically it was the least interesting of the three. He decided on that journey that

Maxie was exactly up his street and that he was going to do it. All he had to do was persuade Dexter and Keeling that he was their man.

He spent the next week scribbling furiously. He took advantage of the studio at the radio station to make a demo tape of his lyrics. Once more he sent off his submission and waited.

One of the lyrics, for *A Clerical Man*, has survived: with Keeling's critical notes scribbled over it, including 'This bit doesn't work at all!', 'Oh, please!' and 'When's he going to stop for breath?' Part of the lyric runs:

VICAR
I am a clerical man.
A sermon, reading your banns,
Your funeral, pastoral care...
These are things that I can handle.
Filing and sorting the mail,
Cross-referencing each detail,
Computer stationery...
They never taught these in the Seminary.

CURATE
Mrs Kissack from 16th Street West
Says pink oleanders suit the chapel best
Or would you prefer some jacaranda
And a fragrant jasmine spray?

VICAR
I think I'll move to L.A.

It was early December 1989 when Keeling phoned to offer McKenna the job. He accepted immediately. He was about to leave Southern Sound to be a freelance writer, with three prospective shows to work on - the Northampton adaptation, a second commission (which subsequently fell through) and *Maxie*.

There was no money in prospect for *Maxie*, no guarantee of production, let alone success, but all three participants felt passionately about the potential of the show. Dexter sent McKenna a copy of the video and they set a start date. *Maxie* was underway.

THE TIME OF MY LIFE

...Crazy kids,
Dressed up and hungry for fame,
Untamed and invincible...

Any writing or performing team will essentially say the same thing: the relationship is like a marriage without sex *[Subsequent experience suggests that it's not always without sex but sex does tend to complicate things].* It needs commitment, space to breathe, the instinct to know where the other person is leading without being told, tolerance, love, trust, understanding and lots of laughs. And like any good relationship, it takes time to build and explore.

In the case of the newly-formed *Maxie* team, there was a three-way relationship to establish. Naturally, the first few meetings at Dexter's flat were slightly tentative. However, all three men were eager to please and eager to establish a rapport with each other. They spent some time round the piano, playing around with the tunes Keeling had written. They generally met on Sundays, for the whole day, when Dexter would cook lunch, giving them informal opportunities to get to know each other better. Sometimes they got sidetracked from the business of adaptation and simply chatted, talking about their lives, comparing the musicals that they loved.

Thinking about *Maxie,* Dexter was reminded of the Marvin Hamlisch/Carole Bayer-Sager *They're Playing Our Song.* This was a small-cast musical that felt like a big, big show, with lots of 'heart' and a rousing Broadway score. It seemed an appropriate genre for the piece they were about to embark on.

All three agreed that the prevailing and fashionable sung-through style (epitomised by *Les Miserables, Miss Saigon, Phantom of the Opera* and *Aspects of Love*) was wrong for *Maxie.* McKenna felt that sung-through scores made comedy (unless very broad) next to impossible - and there were problems in conveying basic information. Singing, 'The doctor has arrived' or 'Would you like a cup of tea?' seemed banal, when dialogue did the job more simply, quickly and effectively.

Fairly soon, the team had established a comfortable working relationship.

Some key decisions were made about *Maxie* early on. It would be a Book musical - ie, the plot would be advanced through dialogue and the characters would sing individual numbers that had a beginning, middle and end. This was a return to what was widely-regarded as an old-fashioned style, certainly one which went against the trend of successful 1980s musicals. It placed *Maxie* in a tradition which went back to *Showboat,* generally regarded as the first modern musical. The sung-through genre, however, had lessons to teach about structure and contemporary staging. Even though the subject was ghostly possession and the loss of identity, the tone would be essentially comic.

It was inevitable that there would be a huge barnstorming dual role for the leading lady, who had to play both Jan Cheyney and the effervescent Maxie. This led naturally to the idea of a big solo show-stopper at the end of Act One - in the manner of *Everything's Coming Up Roses* from *Gypsy* or *Don't Rain On My Parade* from *Funny Girl.* This meant the show would need a star performer. The team excitedly speculated about who might play it, their ambitions bearing no relationship to their pulling power as new writers - names mentioned included Bernadette Peters, Liza Minnelli and even (in an unrestrained flight of fancy) Barbra Streisand, Keeling's idol.

Dexter already had ideas about the book of the show, and this was an area in which McKenna, as a playwright, felt secure. He knew he could write dialogue and scenes whereas, having only ever written the lyrics he had submitted as sample material, he was understandably nervous about writing the songs. At this point, Dexter and Keeling did not know that McKenna was so inexperienced as a lyricist. By the same token, McKenna and Keeling did not know that Dexter had never, in fact, directed anything. This relative inexperience was to prove, in these early stages, a blessing - and fortunately they were all quick learners. All three jumped in with both feet, as if they knew exactly what they were doing. They followed their instincts.

Dexter had established that the film *Maxie* was based on *Marion's Wall,* a novel by American science fiction writer, Jack Finney, most celebrated as the author of *The Invasion of the Body Snatchers* and the cult success, *Time And Again. Marion's Wall* was not easy to locate but Dexter eventually found a copy, which was passed eagerly among the three writers. The team soon discovered that the film, *Maxie,* and the novel, *Marion's Wall* had some radical differences.

Maxie tells the story of Nick and Jan Cheyney (played by Mandy Patinkin and Glenn Close) who are decorating their San Francisco apartment. As they peel off layers of wallpaper, they discover a message - 'Maxie Malone - Read It And Weep.' They are intrigued. All is explained by an eccentric old lady who lives upstairs, Trudi (played by Ruth Gordon). Trudi was once

Maxie's partner in a vaudeville double-act at the old San Francisco Alcazar Theatre. She tells the Cheyneys how the rising star had been killed while making a film in Hollywood - her second film and her first starring role. Nick is intrigued and obtains a copy of Maxie's first film, the only one she ever completed. After watching it one night, the ghost of Maxie appears to him and charms him. A few nights later, Nick and Jan go to a sedate party where Maxie possesses Jan and causes a stir by singing *Bye Bye Blackbird.* Nick drags her away from the party and is subsequently seduced by Maxie in Jan's body. He ends up sleeping with her. Jan, the next day, is horrified when she realises what has happened. Maxie re-possesses Jan and, pursued by Nick, runs away - taking refuge in a cinema. Here she sees a film that uses colour, light and sound (none of which were invented when she was alive) and decides to have another attempt at her career.

Up to this point, the film is broadly faithful to the novel. The screenwriter, Patricia Resnick, calls the dead flapper 'Maxie Malone': in the novel, she is 'Marion Marsh.' Resnick also invents Trudi, who does not appear in Finney's original. In the novel, it is Nick's father who was once romantically involved with Marion Marsh. On a fleeting visit to San Francisco, he tells Nick the story. He does not feature subsequently. In the novel, Nick sells paper products and is a silent movie buff: in the film he is a librarian, being sexually harassed by his boss, and has no special interest in old films. In the novel, Jan is a secretary: in the film she works for the Bishop of San Francisco, giving rise to some broad farce when, possessed by Maxie Malone, she attempts to seduce the Bishop's assistant. It also gives rise to some *Exorcist*-style moments when the Bishop decides to drive out the restless spirit of Maxie.

The film contains a touching moment involving Trudi. The old lady is giving a tap dance class which Maxie, in Jan's body, gatecrashes. Gradually, as Maxie encourages Trudi to talk about her days at the Alcazar Theatre, the old lady realises who she is really talking to - and they have an emotional reunion. Trudi's character is, sadly, largely forgotten after this point.

From the moment where Maxie/Marion decides to re-embark on her career, novel and film diverge widely. In both film and book, though, Jan seems to accept quite calmly the fact that she is being possessed. She allows Maxie/Marion to pursue her dream without this causing much in the way of psychological or marital upset. In *Maxie*, the dead flapper goes to an audition and is cast - she believes she will be making a film. In fact, it is a deodorant commercial based on a *Perils of Pauline*-style scenario. This leads to an opportunity to go to Hollywood, to test for a remake of *Cleopatra*, a role which she obtains before having second thoughts and returning to the ether.

The novel is much darker and more Gothic. Marion makes a ketchup commercial as a Charleston-dancing tomato, which leads on to a small role in a real film. In this film, though, she is required to do a rather seedy nude scene. She stops halfway through and says, in disgust, 'This isn't the movies.' In the closing section of the book, she and Nick trace an ancient Hollywood producer who was the cameraman on the film during which she died, and who was in love with her. He now lives a bizarre, hermit-like existence in the elaborately restored mansion of a dead silent movie star, a shrine to silent pictures. He has an extensive library of lost old movies, including the released version of the film Marion was making when she died. He has cut the last-ever footage of Marion into the completed picture. While he shows it to her in his private cinema, the mansion catches fire. Nick rescues Jan's body but the ghost of Marion Marsh remains, a pale image, hand in hand with her first love, watching her faded film image flickering on the screen. The mansion, its contents and occupants are destroyed. Nick and Jan return to their old life in San Francisco without any significant resulting trauma or personality change.

The novel contains some excellent dialogue and one-liners, many of which were transferred successfully to the film.

Keeling, Dexter and McKenna all agreed that the basic premise shared by film and novel was intriguing and had great comic potential - the possession of Jan by Maxie/Marion, the romantic involvement of Nick with the interloper in Jan's body, and the dead flapper's determination to have another chance at her career. Maxie/Marion was an irrepressible, gutsy, funny and outrageous character who contrasted well with the quieter Jan. The theme was also, clearly, 'Live for today - tomorrow you may be dead,' which tied in with Dexter's original desire for the message of the show.

The team, on balance, was infinitely more attracted to the film version of the story, which seemed to lend itself to musical comedy. The character of Trudi had the potential to be developed into a more significant figure, thus adding a further strand to the piece. The novel's dark and sinister ending was unstageable, except in a multi-million pound production, and even Dexter's unstoppable determination and energy had to admit that the team were unlikely to get that for a first show.
The key issue of obtaining the rights to the source material, without which there could be no show, was discussed. They decided to seek the rights to the screenplay rather than Finney's novel.

There was a lack of communication at this point, one which was to prove crucial in the months and years to come. Each writer thought that another was searching out the rights. As none of them had any available money to purchase an option, it was assumed, wrongly, that a delay in firming up this area would be an advantage.

They started to shape the show, *Maxie*.

◆ ◆ ◆

All three felt that the film was neither tight enough nor funny enough. It took a while to identify exactly where the fundamental weaknesses lay. The first strand to be removed was the subplot concerning the Bishop of San Francisco and his attempts at exorcising the spirit of Maxie. This took up a disproportionate amount of screen time and was silly, rather than comic. One wondered, for example, why Maxie wanted to seduce the unattractive young priest. The comic patter song, which McKenna had set as a sample lyric, was the first song to be cut from the show.

There would be many more.

Dexter had some interesting and imaginative ideas. From the first he was very visually orientated, thinking in terms of how the show might look and how one scene could flow into another. All three writers were determined to avoid front-cloth scenes - scenes which crop up frequently in Rodgers and Hammerstein shows when action takes place in front of a curtain or drop-cloth while the set is being changed behind. These rarely advance the action and often contain reprises of the hit numbers, which serve merely to din the tunes into the audience's memories (The team were only later to appreciate the value of repeating key tunes, so that the audience have heard something often enough that they can leave the theatre humming it). When McKenna joined the team, Dexter and Keeling had been working on a rather grand opening - Trudi leading an *Anthem For A Dead Star*. This would be a memorial service for Maxie at which the great and good of present-day Hollywood lament the disappearance of Maxie and say what a star she would have been. The subsequent story would be a flashback.

If this seems rather reminiscent of *Evita,* it is an indication of how many musicals influenced the team.

Another idea was to set the anthem in 1920s Hollywood. It would finish with young Trudi in the garden of her house, a piece of scenery on a revolving truck. As the years passed, vines and creepers would grow all over it. The truck completed its circle to reveal the now-aged Trudi in the garden as Nick and Jan Cheyney moved in. This was a way of establish the time-lapse and kicking the show off with a big chorale. Keeling had already written a striking *Star* theme.

It was also decided that Nick and Jan's marriage should be seriously threatened by the arrival of Maxie, or the audience would not care what happened to Jan. The team decided to show the marriage in trouble right from the start - the turmoil caused by the possession simply bringing existing underlying tensions to the surface. It was quickly decided to make the party, at which Maxie sings for the first time, a very important event in Nick's business life, to add embarrassment and potential conflict to the brew.

Having discussed ideas at length, it was time to make a start on the writing. McKenna had always found that it was difficult to write onwards unless the first few scenes were in place and the characters securely established, so it was decided to start work on the opening scenes, using the screenplay as a basis. In Scene One, the Cheyneys would uncover the message on the wall and Trudi would fill in the basic story of Maxie Malone. Scene Two would be a split-stage scene in which Nick would be sexually harassed by his superior, Miss Shepherd, while Jan met her friend, Sally, in the gym. A quartet would link the two scenes musically. Scene Three would consist of Nick and Jan watching a video of Maxie's film, the ghost would appear to Nick and he would have a solo number expressing his feelings about the experience.

Keeling and McKenna talked about the tone and style of the songs. They decided that McKenna would draft a lyric for the opening number while Keeling developed the Anthem and wrote the melody for Nick's *Ghost* song. Dexter, meanwhile, would edit the screenplay of the scenes involved, look in detail at the equivalent scenes in the novel and work with McKenna on the dialogue.
All three writers knew that this was crunch time and they had to come up with the goods. They were all excited, and all, in their own ways, terrified.

While the writers worked in their respective homes, a major development took place, one which would irrevocably alter the future of the show - and the writers' careers. Cameron Mackintosh agreed to fund a Visiting Professorship in Contemporary Theatre at St Catherine's College, Oxford. The first visiting professor, during the first half of 1990, was to be Stephen Sondheim. There were twelve places on the course. These would be offered to composers and lyricists whose work, in the opinion of Sondheim and Mackintosh, was sufficiently promising and distinctive. Keeling had been persuaded by Ramin Gray, the director of *The Devil and Mr Stone* to submit a tape of the Donmar warehouse show. Keeling was reluctant - 'If I get turned down by Sondheim, I'll never write another note.' The application date had passed and Gray forced Keeling into the car, drove him to Oxford and made him hand in his submission. Because he submitted it late, when Sondheim finally came to listen to it, all twelve places had been filled. However, so impressed were Sondheim and Mackintosh that they created an extra place and Keeling became the thirteenth participant on the course. *[They subsequently added a fourteenth place for Michael Bland]*

The news of Keeling's acceptance came in early January 1990. The course would be starting within the week. All the participants were asked to bring work-in-progress to Oxford, to be analysed, criticised and developed over a six-month period. While tempted to pursue *The Devil and Mr Stone*, Keeling finally opted to work on *Maxie*.

There was a frantic flurry of activity to get the first three scenes finished in time. Indeed, when McKenna came up with a lyric for the opening song, there was no time for him to hear the music for it until after Keeling had attended the first week of the Oxford course.

This was McKenna's first real lyric and he knew it was going to be presented to Stephen Sondheim! A stimulating challenge. With Dexter, he wrote some dialogue establishing Nick and Jan in the throes of redecorating their apartment. Then he had them gradually burst into song, each beginning with an expository introduction.

Nick began:

The experts tell you jokes and humour
Will keep things in perspective.
But don't be taken in by rumour -
You've got to be selective.
So what if my jokes misfire?
I'm tired, I'm tense,
I'm losing my sense
Of the reasons we're together.
Christ, some nights it seems forever
That we giggled and smoked
And invented the future,
Necking and playing the fool
In the back of the tennis court at school.
Don't be a fool, Nick.

Nothing's the matter.
We're making it, we're fine.
Magic and dreams are for kids.
We're not even slightly on the skids.
We're not even slightly in decline.

Jan continued with an equally long-winded analysis of her emotional state, which ran, in part:

I'm tired, I'm tense.
It's no great offence.
And we know why we're together
And we'll stay that way forever -
Which is how things should be.
We're creating a future.
Things don't work out as you're taught.
Nick and me...

Eventually they came together for a chorus:

There's a moon up there
Trying to look romantic.
It's gigantic and clean and telling us
We have time to spare.
Don't be too ambitious.
It's judicious to count the things we have...
We're making it, we're fine.
Be patient. We have time.

This continued in a similar vein for a couple of pages. McKenna wonders now why he wasn't thrown off the project immediately.

He did better with the quartet, *Eligible Men*. It began with Jan and her friend Sally in the gym. Sally was working with weights while Jan rode an exercise cycle.

SALLY *Honey, isn't exercise a swine!*
JAN *It's worth the pain. It does the trick.*
SALLY *How come you need machines when you've a guy like Nick?*
JAN *It eases stress. You keep in trim.*
SALLY *You could make me very grateful, Jan, by loaning him.*

Where have all the eligible men gone?
That's the cry of women everywhere.
Where have all the eligible men gone?
If you see one, grab him. I'll be there.

The writers had started to explore the possibility that the Cheyney marriage was in trouble because of their failure to have children. As a result, Jan confided to Sally her dismay at being unable to conceive. The scene shifted to the library where Miss Shepherd harassed Nick:

MISS S: *You've a moody, smouldering attraction.*
Clearly you find me attractive too.
NICK *Let's forget it.*
MISS S *Time to take so action.*
NICK *Sorry, but I'm taken.*
MISS S *Well, that just won't do.*

The scene ended with Miss Shepherd and Sally lamenting their enforced celibacy (*Where have all the eligible men gone?*) while Nick and Jan wondered why they were being put under so much pressure. Keeling wrote a driving melody which pulled the scene together.

Scene Three, with the appearance of the ghost, was entirely dialogue as it had been decided that Keeling would write the tune first.

This, plus the opening *Anthem For A Dead Star,* was the material that Keeling took to the first week of the Sondheim master-classes.

A letter he wrote to McKenna at the end of the first week vividly describes the reaction:

> I had a wonderful time in Oxford last week - and Stephen Sondheim is a genius! It's the best word to sum up how I feel about him. As well as going to the National to see rehearsals for *Sunday In The Park With George*, which we are studying as part of the course, we masterclassed our own material - or some of it, to be precise. I did the opening of *Maxie* and I'm afraid it went down like a lead balloon. I'll tell you why. The dialogue Sondheim enjoyed, but had great problems with both the *Hymn* and the proposed opening number, *We're Making It.* He felt they were so gloomy and depressive (particularly the monologues before the main song of *We're Making It*) you wouldn't have a clue the piece was a musical comedy. I played it in front of the students and, sure enough, once into those monologues all attention and interest went out of the room so quickly you wouldn't believe it. I'm afraid it's a No-No - not the scene itself, but the number. We have to rethink *We're Making It* entirely. There is a song to be sung there but we must think again.
>
> I told Steven Dexter and he agrees with me. Nothing is so absolutely final as a disinterested audience! Start again, they said. Dexter and I also think we should scrap the *Hymn* and go for an entirely new Prologue. We think it should be Maxie's farewell party in the flat before she drives off and kills herself. We must meet soon as this needs to be agreed on

> and written if I am to take new stuff back to Oxford. There is a proposed reading at the National theatre *if* the piece is finished, so that's exciting!
>
> Last week we talked so much about lyrics, Shaun and I wish you could have been there. I showed Sondheim your stuff. He felt the rhyming could be better and also the structure. He tore my music apart and I have a lot of thinking to do. That doesn't mean I'm going to drop everything I've written for *Maxie* but I think we have a long way to go. I feel I understand lyrics a whole lot better after just one week of Sondheim. He is very adamant about perfect rhyming. He doesn't tolerate any sort of imperfect rhyming in his own stuff and while I think this rule can be bent a little, it's best to follow it.
>
> Please, please don't think that just because I've met Stephen Sondheim I'm telling you how to write! I realise now, though, *Maxie* is going to take a lot of hard work for us all if we are to get it to a standard where Cameron Mackintosh would consider it.

High hopes were dashed that day, but Sondheim had also said some encouraging things about the potential of the story. He said that to write an American musical comedy was 'just about the hardest thing to do.' He also told Keeling that Mandy Patinkin, whilst filming *Maxie,* had suggested it to him as a potential subject for a musical. The three writers felt that, even if the criticism was searching (even devastating!), it was coming from a master and that things could only improve under his guidance. They set to, and started again.

The first task Sondheim set all the masterclass participants was to write an opening number for their show. As the first two numbers of *Maxie* had just been thrown out, it was a perfect opportunity to start again.

A few days after the above letter, Keeling sent McKenna another letter which was to prove his Bible as he learned about lyric writing and musical structure the hard way:

> I thought I'd send you the notes I made on lyrics during the masterclasses last week:
>
> * Use a perfect rhyme, not a fake rhyme or a near rhyme
> * Be scrupulous about rhyming
> * The best rhyming dictionary is Clement Wood. Avoid Walkers because rhymes are not listed vertically and your eye misses more when laid out horizontally
> * A song should be a perfect marriage of words and music
> * You should be able to justify every note in the music and every word in the lyric
> * 'Very' and 'so' are almost always unnecessary and are generally the work of the amateur
> * Make sure the lyric is always to the point. Know what you are saying and say it concisely.
> * 'Conversational' lyrics should sound as close to the rhythms of natural speech as possible
> * Be careful of filler words (eg, always).
> * Every word in the lyric counts
> * If you're describing someone in a song, make sure you know them very well
> * Don't fall into the trap of *describing* feelings if

you're singing about yourself. You've got to *feel* them - and the lyric must reflect this.

Sondheim's rules for perfect rhymes are:

* The accented syllable *is* the rhyme
* The initial sound (ie, the attack consonant) *must* be different.
* The vowel sound that follows must be *exactly* the same.

This is not printed in any book!!

[Now, of course, Sondheim's notes on lyric writing are included in his two collections, Finishing The Hat *and* Look I Made A Hat *published by Virgin Books. SMcK*]

Unfortunately, the Clement Wood rhyming dictionary was unavailable in the UK. McKenna went through several and found that a combination of Sammy Cahn's *Songwriter's Rhyming Dictionary* (which is American and so needs care when rhyming in standard English) and the tiny Longman *Top Pocket Dictionary of Rhymes* worked well for him.

Dexter, Keeling and McKenna wrote furiously during January and early February 1990. They wrote onwards towards the end of the first act as well as tackling the opening number.

Sondheim had suggested that a new opening number should focus on the wall, as this was where the message would appear. Nick and Jan could make comments about the owners of previous layers of wallpaper, comments which also said something about their own concerns. The writers took this a little too literally and, aware that they also had to say 'This is a musical comedy' with the first number, began with an attempt at easy laughs:

NICK *I'm Nick and Jan's apartment wall.*
I'm nine feet wide and twelve feet tall.
I'm in need of a major overhaul.
Let me tell you 'bout some owners that I recall.

This was a guy called Barrett.
The love of his life was a parrot.
He presented the bird with a lavish bouquet
And whispered sweet nothings to lead it astray
Till two men in white coats came and took him away.
Poor Barrett...

This was a cad called Rudi.
When he danced he was macho and moody.
Strong women would melt in his fervent embrace
As he gripped them and dipped them all over the place
And he died with a permanent grin on his face.
Poor Rudi

The tone got a little more serious (and realistic!) when the invented characters were closer to home:

JAN *This was a girl called Millie.*
Her skin was as pale as a lily.
She struggled and studied and got a degree
But then she found out there was no guarantee
That her life would turn out as she thought it should be.
Poor Millie.

NICK *Here is a guy named Jerry*
Who tried very hard to be merry.
He held down a job and he worshipped his wife,
Was popular, charming and sharp as a knife

But he knew there was more to be got out of life.
Poor Jerry.

Finally the chorus began:

Layer upon layer,
Fragments of lives,
Glimpses of children,
Uncles and wives.
Living day to day,
Not looking very far...
I bet they weren't as happy
As we are...

Never had a problem
We couldn't lick.

JAN *We're always growing.*
Talk to me, Nick.

NICK *Have I said today*
How wonderful you are?

BOTH *How lucky to be happy*
As we are.

Keeling wrote a haunting waltz for the chorus and the three writers felt heartened again. The rhymes were 'perfect' and they felt they had fulfilled Sondheim's brief. Scene One continued as before, with Trudi explaining in dialogue the story of Maxie. Scene Two retained *Eligible Men*. Scene Three briefly had a number for the ghost of Maxie in which she explains what it's like to be dead:

Floating...
Part of the mystery.
Floating...
Pure electricity.
Floating...
One with the universe.

Floating free...

Dexter and Keeling hated this so much that it never got as far as the masterclass. Nick's solo number after the ghost vanishes, *I've Seen A Ghost* was originally titled *I Saw A Ghost* until it was pointed out that it sounded as though he was singing about a ghost named Eyesore.

In its original form, the action during *I've Seen A Ghost* travelled to the library the following day, with Nick continuing to be obsessed with the spirit of Maxie. The party scene followed the screenplay, save for the introduction of another librarian, Mrs Klein. The ensemble were given cocktail party chatter:

Did you catch the Philharmonic?
Could I have a splash more tonic?
What a fabulous complexion!
Has Scorsese changed direction? etc

A song was written in which Maxie jumps on the piano and gets the party going. Originally called *Won't I Make You Blue?*, it was eventually to become *I'll Find Time For You.* Scene Five took place late at night in a children's playground where Nick and Maxie fall in love. Keeling wrote a lyrical romantic melody and McKenna wrote his least clumsy lyric to date:

MAXIE *Feeling this way with you...*
Funny, but I'd forgotten.
Loving the things we do,
Feeling your touch,
Laughing too much with you.
Tasting the air again,
Being aware again,
Knowing the breath of the wind
In my hair again...

Stars shining down
Like the stars I once knew.
Sharing a moment or two

NICK *Feeling this way with you...*
Funny, it seems so easy,
Eager and young and true.
Inside a voice is saying
This is no game we're playing.
Ants in my pants again,
Taking a chance again,
Jumping head first into
Reckless romance again.
MAXIE *Don't let your life slip by.*
NICK *Give me your hand - let's try.*
BOTH *Closer...*
Closer...

Feeling this way with you.
Funny and clean and tender.
Knowing you feel it too.
Fresh as the dawn,
I feel reborn
With you.

The next Sondheim masterclass session on *Maxie* was set for February 28th. This time, Keeling was invited to take McKenna along. He asked whether he could also take Dexter, as the three men were working so closely together, but Sondheim insisted that, for practical reasons, bookwriters were not permitted.

There is a famous saying that 'musicals are not written but re-written.' This was rapidly becoming the *Maxie* team's experience. In response to the often-asked question, 'Which came first? The music or the lyrics?' it is worth looking briefly at the way Keeling, Dexter and McKenna made the collaborative process work.

Everything hinged around long discussions. In some ways, the book of *Maxie* came first, as all three were determined that each of the songs should grow out of the dramatic context and advance the action. The three discussed each scene in detail, working out at which moments the emotions were sufficiently heightened to justify the characters bursting into song. Then a title would be devised to provide the hook for the song. If it was a musical scene or an important plot-driven number, McKenna would generally write the lyric first and send the result to Keeling.

Having started to learn more about song structure, McKenna found himself unable to write a lyric without a tune or rhythm in his head. As he had no skill whatever in composing, he ended up inventing some banal little melody. It was always a surprise when he heard Keeling's musical setting - it bore no resemblance to the melody he had imagined but the tone was always exactly right. He was subsequently delighted to learn from Sondheim that Oscar Hammerstein, who always wrote the words before Rodgers set them to music, used an existing song, brass band march or piece of classical music as a shape for his lyric. He never told anybody what the original tune had been! Keeling had perfect freedom with the lyric - if his melody needed to go in a different direction, McKenna would subsequently re-write to fit.

Big ballads, or numbers for which Keeling already had musical ideas, would be composed before the lyrics were set. This sometimes gave McKenna headaches, as in *I've Seen A Ghost* with its distinctive, jagged-rhythmed short phrases which needed both rhymes and heart. When Keeling and McKenna were finished, the three writers would meet at Dexter's flat and have long sessions round the piano. Dexter revealed a remarkable talent for honing in on any weak spots (both musically and lyrically) and would often come up with inspiring ideas. 'Play that again at half-speed, lose the oom-pah and try a running diddle-diddle-diddle,' was one of his memorable instructions. Frequently it worked.

The party song, which became *I'll Find Time For You* is an interesting example of the collaborative process. Keeling had written a 20s-style sexy blues number that had a very Harlem, black feel. He had researched widely into the music of the period in order to create Maxie's musical context. McKenna listened to the great blues singers, concentrating on the lyrics. He came up with:

My Papa says I'm bad,
The wildest child he's had
But when he treats me like he should
Then I show him I'm real good.
I turn the lamp down low,
I shimmy sweet and slow.
Now, Papa, say you're true
Or won't I make you blue....

Keeling was uncomfortable with the use of 'Papa' - a word frequently used by black singers of the period to refer to their sexual partners - and felt that it gave the song an almost incestuous quality, particularly with lines like *Come here and play, Papa.* Dexter felt that the notion of being 'blue' worked against the song's dramatic imperative to get the party going. There was an hour or more of heated debate. Finally, the pencils came out, the melody was slightly amended, *Honey* substituted for *Papa* and the refrain changed to *I'll find time for you*, which was potentially sexier. It also changed the song from a threat - 'Treat me nice or you're gonna suffer' - to a promise - 'Treat me nice and, boy, will you have a good time!' At the end of the process, all three partners were happy.

A similar process went on when writing the book. At their meetings, the team would go through the existing draft ruthlessly, make changes and come up with ideas. McKenna would go away and re-write, then the process would repeat itself. McKenna and Dexter had many long, late-night telephone conversations about characters and dramatic moments. Sometimes they could not agree and it would take two or three such conversations to reach a happy compromise.

They were all finding that writing a musical comedy was much, much more difficult than they had envisaged.

I'LL FIND TIME FOR YOU

...if he treats me like he should
I'll show him I'm really good.

February 28th 1990, when McKenna went to join Keeling at the Sondheim masterclass, was an unseasonably hot and sunny day. The pair joked that it was a good omen. When McKenna emerged four hours later, he felt as though he had been run over by a tractor!

Sondheim's comments had been no less critical than those he had made the first time round. McKenna was astonished (and heartened) when another of the students, Stephen Clarke, came up and said, 'He obviously likes your work. He didn't give you a hard time at all.' That wasn't how it felt!

In brief, Sondheim had savaged the attempts at cheap humour in the introduction to *As We Are*. He also felt Trudi's story about Maxie, entirely in dialogue, was long and tedious. He suggested musicalising it. He quite enjoyed *Eligible Men* but said firmly that, while it was funny, the characters were two-dimensional. Though it was funny, the show had to decide on its style. Was it to be a thoughtful musical about a couple struggling to come to terms with the difficulties in their lives, or an up-front, fast-moving farce in the style of George Abbott? He suggested that the team go away and think long and hard about this. *Ghost* and Maxie's party song went down quite well but it was felt that a party chorus was both obvious and hackneyed. There was much discussion about the love duet, *Feeling This Way With You*. The consensus was that it was too soon for Nick to fall in love with Maxie - or at least that there was insufficient build-up to a fully fledged romantic ballad. He thought this was the right place for a number but that it should be a song about the pair of them having fun.

The team went back to the drawing board, though encouraged by Sondheim's assertion that he thought the show had the potential to get on. They added a choreographed Prologue in which Maxie is seen dancing on the stage of the Alcazar Theatre, receiving a phone call, writing 'Read It And Weep' on the apartment wall in lipstick, travelling to the train station and waving goodbye to Trudi. The train crash is heard and Trudi, sadly, exits. This was largely Dexter's inspiration - a fluid, fast-moving up-tempo sequence that was visually interesting, established a musical comedy genre and told us a story which Trudi could recap more briefly later.

As We Are was pruned of its more embarrassing moments and bedded more firmly into the scene. When Trudi was telling the story of Maxie, it recurred as a trio (Trudi, Jan, Nick). Trudi sang about life with her late friend, *As We Were*:

Dancing on tables,
Painting our toes,
Out on the razz with
Handsome young beaux.
Faces rushing by
Till life became a blur.
We never called it happy
But we were.

Scene Two remained as *Eligible Men*. Concerned by Sondheim's comments about the characterisations, the team decided to dispense with Miss Shepherd, Nick's boss. Dexter came up with the idea of a grand society hostess, Mrs van Gelder. She was conceived as a wealthy widow, patroness of the library, and perhaps slightly vulgar - she may have been a starlet in her former life. Having been without love for a long time, Mrs van Gelder would take a fancy to Nick and use her influence to have her wicked way with him. This partly picked up on the film's notion of Nick being sexually harassed by his boss, but the character was conceived in much grander, more dangerous terms. It also established that Nick was faithful to Jan, whatever their problems, and was not the sort of man to have a quick fling. This makes his subsequent capitulation to Maxie much more resonant. The name Mrs van Gelder was later changed to Mrs van Arc as the original was felt to be too close to Horace Vandergelder in *Hello Dolly*.

Scenes Three and Four (the 'ghost' scene and the party) remained much as they had been, and the love duet was replaced by a new, more up-tempo number, *Swinging High*, while Nick and Maxie played on the apparatus in a children's playground:

Swinging high,
Swinging low,
Death-defying
It's flying we go...
This sensation's nearly
The best I know.
I'd forgotten how it
Make you glow.
I tell ya,
I could swing like like this forever,
Never let it go, ' cos when you're
Swinging high,

Swinging low
That's when, baby, you know you're alive...

For the first time, the team tackled the 'morning after' scene when Jan briefly resurfaces before being taken over once more by Maxie, who is subsequently reunited with Trudi. This was a purely musical moment: Trudi reprised their old Alcazar routine, Maxie joined in and Trudi realised who she was.

The next scene was rather bolder, and very much in the broad musical comedy genre. The writers conceived a comic therapy group, run by Sally. Sally invites Jan to join the group during *Eligible Men* and, later, distraught by Nick's betrayal, she runs to Sally for sanctuary. She arrives in the middle of a group session, which is peopled by an assortment of bizarre misfits and weirdos. Some crisp, funny dialogue leads to the ensemble launching into the manic *Blame It On Mama*, parodying the perception of some Freudian analysts that most traumas can be laid at the door of one's parents (also touching on re-birthing and primal screaming).

All three writers had reservations but the scene *was* very funny and Keeling had written a dynamic, driving tune. They decided to wait for Sondheim's reaction.

The final scene of Act One was set outside a cinema in downtown San Francisco, where Nick attempts a reconciliation with Jan. She becomes upset and, to avoid him, runs into the cinema. Maxie emerges to sing her projected show-stopper, *Star:*

No-one ever told me there was sound!
Say, how long has colour been around.
Right away I knew it, at a glance,
This is my chance!
Nothing's gonna stop me -
Not now!

This song, like *I'll Find Time For You* and *Ghost*, found its shape and form very quickly. It has remained in the show in something very close to its original incarnation. *Star* gave Keeling the opportunity to revive the key theme from the now-deleted *Anthem* - Sondheim was always adamant that nothing good should be allowed to go to waste, even if it had proved unsuitable in its original placement. Keeling took the *Star* theme for the chorus and added a pounding, driving verse section, which McKenna subsequently set.

When Keeling and McKenna returned to the final masterclass session on *Maxie* on April 25th, they were confident that huge progress had been made. Sondheim agreed, though he still had some major reservations. He felt that the opening scene was still slow and that *As We Are* still did not sit entirely comfortably. *Swinging High* was better than the love duet but still not energetic enough. He had some problems with *Star* because he felt it was too reminiscent of his own *Everything's Coming Up Roses*. This was an area where the writers would never entirely agree with him. They felt that *Roses* was in itself part of a tradition of big belters and that they were justified in using the genre.

As to *Blame It On Mama*, Sondheim laughed a lot and enjoyed the song. He then said, categorically, that it was a song from an entirely different show and had no place in *Maxie*. He felt that the style of the show was still fragmented, with *Mama* and *Eligible Men* pulling in one direction and the more serious and realistic Nick and Jan story pulling in quite another. He called the piece, 'seriously schizophrenic.'

It was extraordinary, though, to glimpse something of the way his mind worked. Attention to detail was supreme and Sondheim could remember, word for word, lyrics that he had heard only once, two months before. He would ask, for example, why a particular word had been changed and explain in detail why another word was better. Both writers began to understand why his own work was so intricate and multi-layered.

They were also determined not to fall into the trap that some of the other course participants were showing signs of - trying to write like Sondheim. There was no point. Sondheim did it better. They were determined to establish a style of their own.

◆ ◆ ◆

Slightly to Keeling's frustration, the majority of the time on the Sondheim course was spent talking about lyrics. Sondheim referred to composing as the 'fun bit that comes at the end.' Nevertheless, Keeling learned some valuable lessons about composing for the theatre.

Sondheim criticised Keeling's sense of musical structure - which he said had a tendency to ramble - and encouraged him to work on song form. He suggested that Keeling go back to the beginning and look at the 32-bar song. This is the earliest (and classic) American musical theatre song style and basically consists of a clear AABA structure, in groups of eight bars - ie, chorus, chorus, middle eight, chorus. Sondheim felt that this would be the right form for *Maxie* though, of course, once established the basic form could be extended and adapted.
One of the key musical ideas for *Maxie* arose from the contrast between Maxie's jazzy 1920s style and the more modern style of the Cheyneys. Keeling's intention was to have most of Maxie's early songs in a pastiche 1920s style, becoming more up to date and Broadway as she grew, learned and progressed. Eventually the two styles would merge and pastiche would be left behind.

An *Omnibus* TV documentary was shot during the master-classes and rehearsals for *Sunday In The Park*. This contains some interesting comments by Sondheim, including:

> The test of a show is to be able to do it in a room like this with just tables, chairs and an audience with an imagination... Intelligibility is the most important thing. Consider your audience without pandering to them. Recognise their sensibilities. The audience is the final collaborator.

◆ ◆ ◆

With McKenna and Keeling working closely together, in isolation from Dexter, the balance of the writing team was changing. Dexter was uncomfortable about being excluded from the masterclasses, and felt that instructions were coming back to him, without him being party to the discussions which gave rise to them. The speed at which the first act was re-written - often by Keeling and McKenna - also meant that he had not had time to fully digest where the show was heading. This tension was slightly eased when he went to work at the National Theatre as a stage manager (on Tony Harrison's *Trackers of Oxyrhyncus*). Now he could be around *Sunday In The Park* rehearsals, meet Sondheim and get to know some of the other course participants. Dexter felt that working at the National was a logical step in his move towards directing. He had worked on a West End musical and a West End play and he valued the opportunity to observe at first hand the directing process at such a centre of excellence. Someone had once said to him, 'A good stage manager is always one step ahead of the director' and Dexter was determined to learn as much as he could from being a fly on the wall. He had also, by this time, found an agent - Mark Hudson - who was to influence events greatly in the ensuing months.

However, he was feeling insecure about his role in the writing team - he rarely did any physical writing at this stage, but came up with ideas - and started to worry that he was being nudged out. He remembers clearly a conversation with McKenna and

Keeling in which it was mooted that *Maxie* might be picked up by a big producer and Dexter might not be allowed to direct it. Dexter felt that *Maxie* was his baby and he had to hold on to it.

[In retrospect, I wasn't nearly sensitive enough to Stephen's concerns. I just smelled the chance of the show being a hit. I regret not thinking about his feelings - it would contribute greatly to the dramas that followed. SMcK]

◆ ◆ ◆

In June, at the end of the masterclasses, most of the students felt that they were on a fast track and were going to get their work produced in the foreseeable future. Each of the participants was given the opportunity to present a thirty minute excerpt of the work in progress. This was the perfect opportunity for Dexter to take hold of the project again - and, more importantly, to show his directing skills. He says now, 'As a young, hungry, ambitious wannabe director who hadn't directed anything, I jumped on that opportunity and flew with it.' He knew a number of the *Sunday In The Park* company, and approached other established West End players. Within a few days it was cast and ready to go. The central role of Jan/Maxie was offered to Denise Wharmby, a former member of *Fascinating Aida*, and a participant in the masterclasses. Nicolas Colicos was Nick, Janie Dee the ghost of Maxie, Ria Jones played Sally and Mary Millar Mrs van Arc. Matt Zimmerman was recruited to narrate a truncated version of the first act and play a comic senator in the party scene and Vivienne Martin made a brief appearance doubling as Trudi and Mrs Klein. Nigel Denham, Caroline Harding and John Arnott generously agreed to play tiny roles. Sarah Newall stage managed.

[Looked at twenty five years on, this was a cast to die for! Dexter always had brilliant casting taste. SMcK]

The team decided to showcase *Maxie's* strengths. The first scene (which was still unresolved and uncomfortable) was cut entirely and narration linked into *Eligible Men*. There followed the appearance of the ghost, Nick's *Ghost* song, and the comic party, climaxing with Maxie's *I'll Find Time For You* on top of the piano. A short narration linked through to Maxie's big number, *Star* (which was then called *Nothing's Going To Stop Me*).

What Keeling failed to tell Dexter was that the showcase was only intended to be a very simple presentation. Cameron Mackintosh was to employ a pool of actors, to be used by all the writing teams to present their work. This pool would include John Barr, Clare Burt, Michael Cantwell, Mario Frangoulis, Glyn Kerslake, Grace Kinirons, Paul Leonard and Matthew White. However, having gone so far with casting *Maxie*, there was no going back. Rehearsals took place at Pineapple Studios in Covent Garden. Dexter staged the scenes fluidly and wittily. He betrayed no sign of nerves, though he was terrified. The presentation was to be on June 8th at the Holywell Music Room, St Catherine's College, Oxford.

McKenna was unable to attend. He was mortified. He had found that being a freelance writer was not providing sufficient income to live. He was temping for American Express in Brighton and working odd days as a freelance speech and drama examiner for LAMDA. The Oxford presentation came two days into a ten-day long LAMDA tour of Scotland. He was unable to cancel the day without cancelling the whole tour, and he could not afford to do that. So, with very mixed feelings, he wished the company luck, sent cards and drove north.

June 8th was a very big day for *Maxie*. The company trekked up to Oxford in the morning, had a quick run-through and prepared for the performance. It is fair to say that there was a measure of resentment from some of the other participants because the *Maxie* team had largely ignored the pool of actors and, in addition, were working without scripts.

The audience was full of big theatre names and people of influence - including not only Stephen Sondheim and Cameron Mackintosh but Lionel Bart and Peter Nichols. *Maxie*'s turn came.

It is no exaggeration to say that the audience went wild. Both audio and video recordings survive from the event.

[Video can be found on YouTube -

https://www.youtube.com/watch?v=DJMKWMuGxDO]

The story captured their interest. People laughed at the jokes, both in the dialogue and the lyrics. The tunes caught their imagination and the ovation at the end was tremendous. Keeling was playing the piano, so had to concentrate on the music rather than the audience reaction. Dexter was so nervous that he remembers very little about the performance itself - but it is clear from the tapes that Mary Millar stole the show as the voluptuous Mrs van Arc, Nic Colicos made a charmingly hangdog Nick and Janie Dee a convincingly sensual ghost of Maxie. Denise Wharmby was an excellent Jan but the big belt numbers for Maxie did not entirely suit her voice. Nevertheless, *Maxie* was one of the two stand-out shows in the presentation, together with Kit Hesketh-Harvey and James McConnell's fable of pre-Revolutionary Russia, *Yusupov*.

By the end of that day, the project was rolling. *Maxie* had been noticed and so had Dexter. It was the day his career as a director really began.

After the presentation, Cameron Mackintosh approached Dexter and said, 'Get the cast down to twelve and we'll do the show at the Watermill, Newbury. It's exactly the show we've been looking for.' Dexter could not believe his ears. He had huge admiration for Mackintosh's achievements and had once spoken briefly to him at a *Follies* after-show party. Now it looked as though the world's most successful theatre producer was going to pick up *Maxie.* At that time, Mackintosh was working closely with Jill Fraser at the Watermill and had tried out some new shows there - including George Stiles and Anthony Drewe's *Just So.* It was a perfect venue for *Maxie* to start life.

The team's wildest dreams were coming true. Dexter was so flabbergasted by it all that he asked McKenna's agent, who was in the audience, to speak to Mackintosh to confirm what he had just said. She did, and Mackintosh confirmed that, subject to the quality of the finished script, he *was* interested in backing a Newbury production.

Then it was back to reality. There was a 'post-mortem' after the showcase and Dexter felt very awkward and uncomfortable. Sondheim was a little taken aback by just how rapturous the reception had been and Dexter was very aware that, because Keeling had not emphasised the simplicity of the brief, his had been the most sophisticated presentation. He felt as though he had vast amounts of egg on his face for having 'barged in with a big West End cast.'

◆ ◆ ◆

Having attracted such a positive and powerful response, and now believing that *Maxie* had a real chance, the team realised that they still hadn't acquired the rights to *Marion's Wall.* They urgently needed to do so or the whole project could die on its feet. McKenna's agent, Rachel Daniels, undertook this task. Unexpectedly, this turned into *Maxie*'s first big hurdle.

[To any aspiring adapters reading this - GET THE RIGHTS TIED UP FIRST!!!! If that is not entirely clear, <u>GET THE RIGHTS TIED UP FIRST!!!!</u> ***GET THE RIGHTS TIED UP FIRST!!!!]***

The rights to the *Maxie* screenplay were owned by Orion Films and had been sold on as part of a complicated package. It would be expensive and time-consuming to track them down. What was clear, however, was that obtaining the screenplay rights would also involve obtaining the rights to *Marion's Wall*, as this remained the original source material. None of the writers had any money - indeed, McKenna was almost facing bankruptcy - and the prospect of finding even small option payments for two sets of rights was daunting. Daniels pursued the novel rights first, contacting Don Congdon, Jack Finney's New York-based agent.

Congdon came back with an unenthusiastic response. Finney had always hated adaptations of his work, even the classic 1950s Don Siegel film of *Invasion of the Body Snatchers.* He was far from keen on the idea of a musical. However, Congdon *was* prepared to agree to selling an option, on one condition: Finney had so loathed the film *Maxie* that nothing was to be used from it (unless the material had also appeared in the original novel). Finney also wanted script approval.

Daniels fired back a letter asking Finney to relent on several substantive points. She managed to quash the script approval condition but was unable to get him to budge on the use of material from the film. It meant that there was now no need to obtain rights to the screenplay but it left the writers with a big problem - up until this point they had based their development on the film.

Back to the drawing board again.

In the meantime, in the wake of the success of the Oxford presentation and as a result of the media and theatre-world interest that had arisen from the Sondheim masterclasses, there was to be a repeat presentation at the Lilian Baylis Theatre,

Sadlers Wells, on July 27th. The team had already started frantic reworking of the show but felt that it would be too risky to put the untried changes into such an important showcase. Instead, they repeated the formula that had proved so successful at Oxford.

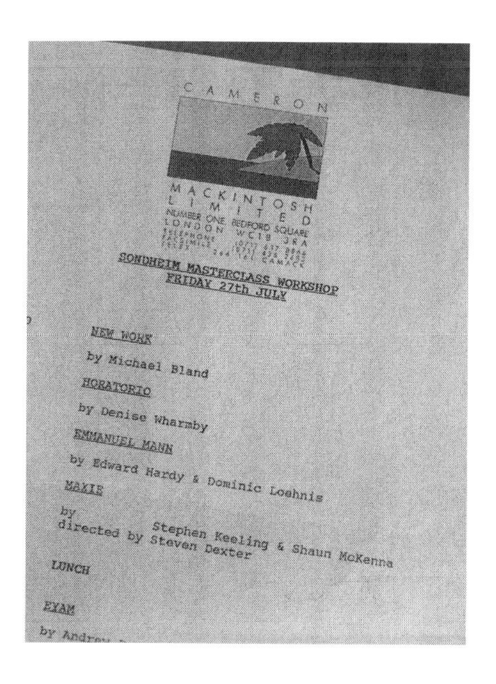
CAMERON MACKINTOSH LIMITED
NUMBER ONE BEDFORD SQUARE
LONDON WC1B 3RA

SONDHEIM MASTERCLASS WORKSHOP
FRIDAY 27th JULY

NEW WORK
by Michael Bland
HORATORIO
by Denise Wharmby
EMMANUEL MANN
by Edward Hardy & Dominic Loehnis
MAXIE
by Stephen Keeling & Shaun McKenna
directed by Steven Dexter

LUNCH

EXAM
by Andrew

There were some cast changes. Caroline O'Connor played Jan/ Maxie, Vivienne Martin was unavailable and was replaced by Stella Tanner and Nicola Blackman took over from Ria Jones as Sally. Otherwise, the team remained intact. Caroline O'Connor was a great asset. At the time she had a tremendous reputation within the industry but was little known by the general public. She always seemed to end up playing second leads in big shows (and stealing the notices!). She was a gifted comedienne and had a glorious, gutsy belting singing voice. When she sang 'I'll be a star!' you knew that one day she would.

Once again, with Dexter's fluid direction, *Maxie* caused a stir. Jill Fraser from the Watermill Theatre in Newbury attended and liked what she saw. A few days later, the team were invited down to the Watermill for an informal barbecue (with Wendy Toye and George Stiles) and to talk further. The team even went swimming in the mill-pond. Jill asked for a completed script by the end of September. If she liked that, a production in Spring 1991 was a serious possibility.

Stephen and Shaun at Newbury, the day of the barbeque

For the team, the whole period was extraordinary. To have their work acknowledged by such important figures in the industry was a tremendous boost. Dexter in particular felt that at last he was being validated, that people he had always admired and respected were saying, 'Yes, you can be one of us.'

There was a great deal of work to be done. Not only did every trace of the film have to be removed from the show, but the second act did not yet exist - though there were some ideas for a few numbers.

Two major changes had to be addressed. The film's 'Maxie Malone' had been rechristened 'Maxie Marsh' but now her forename had to be changed as well. This was harder than it seemed. The name 'Maxie' sounded Twenties, the sound of it was gutsy and up-front and the central 'X' sound gave it bite. The novel's 'Marion' had none of these qualities. The alliteration of a name with two Ms was felt to be attractive. The team spent a whole afternoon exploring alternatives - Maxine Marsh, Millie Marsh, Maisie Marsh, Mavis Marsh, Margo Marsh, Melinda Marsh, Roxie Rogers - none of them felt right or were too similar to leading characters in other shows.

When Keeling first suggested 'Maddie,' McKenna and Dexter dismissed it. However, they kept coming back to it. 'Maddie' is a more ladylike name than 'Maxie' - less vulgar and brassy. As they talked through the new plot developments, it occurred to them that it was an opportunity to keep the energy and excitement of Maxie while giving her a softer, more sympathetic side. 'Maxie' began to feel like a caricature, whereas 'Maddie' became a real, three-dimensional person. Finney's insistence on leaving the film behind, which at first seemed such a blow, came to be seen as a blessing.

The other big problem was Trudi – 'Trudi Lisco, the toast of 'Frisco,' Maxie's old cabaret partner. There was no doubt that she had to go, but the team loved the notion that someone from Maddie's past would remember her. Dexter re-read the book. He picked up on the aged cameraman who had been Marion's first love. This was a seam even richer than an old vaudeville partner - it added a second love story and the old man's potential jealousy of Nick to the mix. McKenna re-read the novel, too, and thought about the transient figure of Nick's father, who first relates Marion's story. The two were combined. It was a small adjustment to have Nick and Jan moving into the top floor of Nick's father's house, a house he had bought because Maddie once lived there. Nick's father was nameless in the novel. In the novel, the Cheyneys own a dog called Al. McKenna put the two together and Nick's father became Al. It reminded him of the old song *Buddy, Can You Spare A Dime:*

> *Say, don't you remember, they called me Al,*
> *It was 'Al' all the time.*

It had the right 1920s feel.

For the rest, the structure of the first act was well-established and seemed to work. Picking up on the last batch of masterclass comments gave the team some guidelines for further changes. *Ghost, Star* and *I'll Find Time For You* worked and were largely left alone. Mrs van Arc had already developed in a different direction to the film's Miss Shepherd and it was a simply a question of changing one or two lines of dialogue. Every other element was drawn from the novel.

As We Are was junked as the opening number for Nick and Jan but the reprise, *As We Were*, became Al's song of reminiscence about Maddie later in the scene. A new opening number was created, still based around the wall but enabling Nick and Jan to be more at odds with each other. It was called *Just This Wall.* This draft emphasised Jan's childless state as the primary source of conflict, giving her an overdeveloped sense of fear about Nick leaving her. The idea was that at the very end of the show, Jan would discover she was pregnant (Maddie's presence having somehow cleared her internal problems) and there would be the suggestion that Maddie would be reincarnated as the baby.

The action continued as before until *Swinging High.* Keeling wrote an entirely new Charleston-style tune, which was set as the more active *Swing Me High.* As well as taking place in a playground on the night of Mrs van Arc's party, it was reprised in the morning after scene, when Maddie attempted to seduce Nick for the second time:

MADDIE *Swing me high!*
NICK *Thanks, I'll pass.*
MADDIE *You're a cuddly guy*
With the cutest ass!
Last night showed me
That you're, boy!, world class.
I tell ya
We could swing like that forever,
Life would be a gas...

Al's reunion with Maddie remained entirely musical.

The therapy scene was cut in its entirety. Instead, Jan arrives at Sally's flat and they sing a duet, *I'm Never Gonna Speak To Him Again:*

JAN *Don't ask me to forgive him.*
SALLY *I never said a word.*
JAN *Don't know why I thought he'd take it.*
SALLY *But what's happened?*
JAN *It's absurd!*
He's tossed away our marriage,
He's ruined every plan.
He's a no-good selfish bastard.
SALLY *He's a man.*
JAN *Boy, I'm gonna make him suffer.*
He thinks Maddie's tough, I'm tougher.
I'm no doormat he can walk on.
SALLY *Oh, amen.*
JAN *I am never gonna speak to him again...*

The attempted reconciliation scene occurred outside the cinema, leading to *Star.*

The team had never forgotten the first tune Keeling composed for the show (which was to become *Time of My Life*). They opened Act Two in Al's apartment. Here Maddie, having gate-crashed an audition for tango dancers, comes to ask Al to persuade Jan to allow her to use her body in order to make a film. This seemed a perfect moment for Al and Maddie to reminisce, which they did, using the tune. This version was called *Two Crazy Kids*. Jan agrees to Maddie's proposals and the action moves to the filming - a commercial for deodorant. Maddie is an exotic Eastern temptress who rejects all her suitors because they do not smell good enough for her. *The Chic Sheik* was a tango.

Maddie, discovering the movie she thought she was making is a deodorant commercial, vanishes - leaving Jan to make a mess of the carefully rehearsed routine. This sequence is in another great tradition of the hopeless amateur making a comic mess of a dance routine - Streisand on roller skates in the film of *Funny Girl* or Julie Andrews with puttees and a rifle in *Star!*

The next sequence came together quite quickly and, again, has retained much of its original form. Jan declares her independence from Maddie in the rousing *From Now On,* and declares her intention to leave Nick. He responds with a desperate plea, *Afraid.*

Keeling wrote the music for *Afraid* first and sent a tape to McKenna who was still living in Brighton. McKenna's wife, Jenny, had been chronically sick for nine months since collapsing with a mystery illness. They were in grave financial difficulties, trying to feed themselves on three pounds a day and facing the possibility of losing their flat. The stress of it all was causing difficulties in their relationship. Jenny was bed-ridden and could barely get to the bathroom - otherwise, she would have left him. The situation seemed, in some ways, to mirror Nick's. Late one night, after a particularly difficult day, McKenna sat at the kitchen table to set the lyric to Keeling's haunting tune:

I know it's frightening
When you lose the things you've known.
The net is tightening
And it feels like you're alone.
But, if you'll let me,
I'll be your rock.
I'll hold you steady when you reel from every shock.

You think the world is falling down,
You think it's more than you can bear,
You're lost and helpless in the storm.
Don't be afraid.
I'm always there.
When you can't sleep because you're scared,
When you can't face another day,
I'll be your lantern in the dark.
Don't be afraid.
I'll find the way.
Don't be afraid.

Sondheim was in London for the rehearsals of the first London production of *Into The Woods* and Keeling had arranged to see him for a private session on the new material. Sondheim had some interesting and pertinent criticisms to make of the other songs and said that he felt *Afraid* was, musically, the best thing Keeling had ever written. He didn't like the lyric at all, though, thinking the images clichéd and the tone too self-conciously poetic and old fashioned. 'Not up to Shaun's usual standard,' he said - which was a grain of comfort.

Having written it in an emotional moment and with great sincerity, McKenna felt a little flattened. However, he took the criticism on board and sat back down at the kitchen table. Again, it was the middle of the night. His circumstances had deteriorated further since the first version and he decided that the way forward was to be as honest and simple as he could. The result has never been changed:

We seemed so perfect at the start.
There's not a thought we couldn't share.
I didn't see us grow apart.
Now I'm afraid
But I still care.
Think I don't understand your fears?
That sense that life is slipping by...
Please don't give up on seven years.
Don't be afraid.
At least let's try.
I'm not afraid.

McKenna was subsequently to give his wife, who stayed with him, the royalties on this song. *[A romantic gesture, I suppose, but rather an empty one. There were never any royalties. SMcK]*

Having reached this point in the story, the team suddenly hit a block. Maddie was expelled from Jan's body and floating invisibly around the apartment, Nick and Jan's marriage was on the rocks and nobody knew what to do with Al. The Newbury deadline was fast approaching and they had to find a conclusion to the story. They spent two whole days in Dexter's apartment trying to find a solution.

In the end, they picked up on the darker tone of the novel's conclusion. A telephone call for Jan came from someone who had seen the commercial and she was invited to a screen test in Hollywood. As she had turned her back on the life she knew, she accepted the offer. Nick went after her, trying to save his marriage. The unseen spirit of Maddie also pursued her, behaving like a poltergeist and developing telekinetic powers. As

Jan attempted the screen test, the power suddenly went off in the studio and the ghost of Maddie appeared. She became agitated and declared, 'This isn't the movies!' before supernaturally wrecking the studio. Jan and Nick were finally reconciled.

This ending had a 'mad scene' for the ghost of Maddie not a million miles away from the end of Billy Wilder's film, *Sunset Boulevard.* At that point, Andrew Lloyd Webber's musical version of *Sunset* had not yet appeared and the team simply prayed that they would get their show on first.

[See? Young, naive, optimistic. Rather than solving the problem we hoped it would go away. SMcK]

The script was printed and despatched to Newbury, along with a very rough demo tape sung by the three writers. The team awaited Jill Fraser's response.

It took a week. It was a firm, 'No, thank you.'

FROM NOW ON

From now on I don't care what you threaten,
From now on no-one pushes me around...

All three writers pretended that it did not matter that Newbury had turned down the show but in their hearts they were bitterly disappointed. They now understood that getting a new musical, by new writers, produced anywhere, let alone the West End, was akin to climbing Everest. Up to now, they had felt that they were quickly ascending to base camp. Now they were back at the very foot of the mountain and, it seemed, had no guides.

They did not stop believing, but there was a definite slump. Jill Fraser had hated the ending, and was also unhappy about both Nick and Al, his father, having a sexual relationship with Maddie. She felt that it brought a rather seedy, almost incestuous, feeling to the piece which she found distasteful - and which would certainly not appeal to Newbury audiences.

The writers took these comments on the chin and followed Jerome Kern and Dorothy Fields' advice: they picked themselves up, dusted themselves off and started all over again. It was hard slog - the urgency had gone out of the project. They had no deadline to work to and all their existing contacts had effectively declined the piece.

Dexter resolved this problem. Working at the National Theatre, he was aware of the National Theatre Studio, where new writing projects were explored and workshopped using members of the

National Theatre Company. He approached the administrator, Sue Higginson. She was interested - it would be the first time the National had undertaken a workshop on a new musical. Tentative dates were set for Spring 1991.

McKenna, more disheartened than he admitted even to himself, was unsure of the value of undertaking another workshop. He felt that they had already been down that route without success. However, he allowed Dexter and Keeling's enthusiasm to persuade him. At least it gave them something to work towards.

During November and December 1990, the team embarked furiously on rewrites. McKenna's life was not in good shape. He was broke, his wife was chronically ill and showed no signs of getting better. He was temping in Brighton and having to cram all the *Maddie* rewrites into evenings and weekends, which, with the care his wife required, was increasingly difficult. However, *Maddie* at this point was all he had to hold on to as a potential way of earning some money and getting them out of the hole they were in. While his Northampton adaptation of *How Green was My Valley* had been very well-received, other writing commissions were thin on the ground.

The team set to work. They decided that the incestuous element would be removed if Al was Nick's grandfather. They decided to lose all reference to the Cheyneys' childless state as the source of their marital difficulties.

The biggest problem was the development of Act Two after Nick's big ballad, *Afraid.* They kicked ideas around for a couple of weeks, in meetings and long phone calls. What would Maddie do next? What *could* she do? She had been thrown out of Jan's body and was a disembodied spirit. She had to have another body to get to Hollywood to do the screen test. Was there anyone else she could possess?

None of the minor characters from Act One participated in the second half of Maddie's story. The writers considered Nick, but that would have ended up with the leading actor in drag, and would make the Cheyneys' relationship almost impossible to resolve. They considered the possibility of Maddie possessing Al - but that would have been even more ludicrous. A passing stranger? The postman?

It was Keeling who came up with the brilliantly obvious but unexpected idea of Maddie possessing Mrs van Arc. Hitherto, Mrs van Arc had been simply a minor character with a couple of good scenes. Mary Millar had given a wonderful performance in the Oxford and London workshops, creating a memorable character. The team had wanted to exploit her further but had been unable to work out how. Now Keeling's suggestion had killed two birds with one stone.

It was a straightforward plot development, Mrs van Arc having arranged Nick's dismissal from the museum, to have her return at the key moment with an offer of reinstatement in return for sexual favours. But how would the possession take place?

The team had always wanted to ensure that Maddie's extraordinary story was grounded in reality. Nick and Jan's relationship had been written with sensitivity and layers of subtext. The magical elements had been carefully introduced. Even van Arc, in her latest incarnation, had credible motivation and more than two dimensions. The subject of the mechanics of ghostly possession had been discussed at length, to ensure that the script provided credible and logical rules regarding the supernatural elements.

The magic does not begin until the lipstick message is uncovered. Jan touches the wall at the end of Scene One and wishes she knew how it felt to be Maddie. The message glows, establishing contact with Jan - and nobody else. Maddie herself, when appearing as a ghost, says:

> 'We can come back to where we once lived, you know, but it takes a lot of juice... I can't stay long, sheik. This ectoplasm stuff is kinda tricky... The only way to stick around for any length of time is by possession, but you'd have to want something real bad.'

During the morning after scene, Maddie explains how she managed to possess Jan:

> 'This is my room. It's the only place I can get through. (*points to the message*) See? Her thinking about me, wishing she was like me... I used that energy.'

In later drafts, this was refined to make the point clearer and stronger. Maddie says to Nick:

> 'She was in my room. She touched my message. That's how I got through. She wanted to know how it felt to be me. Whoo! I was so lucky! All those forces, all at once. My movie, in my room. My message on the wall. Jan. And, of course, you!.... You fell in love with me at first sight. That gave me the extra kick I needed. All that lovely energy.'

It was felt that Maddie's power over Jan would grow stronger the longer she was in possession. However, early in Act Two, Maddie reveals to Al that perhaps she is not all-powerful. If she doesn't "hold on tight", Jan could get back in and wreck her comeback before it has even started.

All the writers had to do, to make the re-possession of Mrs van

Arc work, was to establish that the spirit of Maddie, driven out of Jan's body, was still present. This was achieved with a simple disembodied voice, a device already established during the number *From Now On*. Then Mrs van Arc has to touch the message on the wall. She sarcastically admires Nick's decor, commenting, 'Oh how quaint! You have graffiti, too!.' She reaches out and, touching the message, she makes contact - the words glow and she is possessed by Maddie.

The beauty of this is that it takes the show in an entirely new and unexpected direction, with enormous comic possibilities. The writers seized on them eagerly, Keeling's idea giving their inspiration a kick in exactly the place it was needed. Maddie/ Mrs van Arc was given a reprise of *Star*, McKenna wrote a funny scene at the studio gates and in the final confrontation between Jan and Maddie, Maddie was able to reveal a softer, more desperate side in her emotional appeal to Jan, *If Not For Me*:

If not for me,
Would you have seen
That your marriage was dying?
If not for me,
Would there have been
This chance to pull through...?

There were several associated benefits. The role of Mrs van Arc became much richer and more significant - a role which might now attract an older star performer. It also helped an ever-present worry about the number of songs which were sung by either Jan or Maddie. Though they were different characters, they were the same performer. There was a danger that the audience might think, 'Here she goes again!'

With the second half of Act Two now firmly in place, attention was given to the remainder of the script. The structure was sound - and, indeed, has not been changed significantly in the succeeding years. Al's version of *As We Were* was replaced by a new song telling Maddie's 1920s story, *Maddie, Dancing*, another song which found a place in the writers' hearts and has changed little. Al and Maddie's song of reminiscence in Act Two Scene One, *Two Crazy Kids*, was too downbeat as the first number after the interval. It found its home, and new title, *Time of My Life*, at the moment of their reconciliation in Act One. A new, up-tempo number was written for the first scene of Act Two, *One More Day*, in which Maddie asks Al to persuade Jan to let her make the commercial. The commercial itself became an ad for chilli sauce, based on the famous tango scene in Valentino's silent film, *Four Horsemen of the Apocalypse*. This moment seemed like such a splendid opportunity for a comic song that the writers ignored the reservations which told them that a TV commercial would be forty seconds long, at most.

The script was now felt to be ready for the National Theatre Studio workshop, which Dexter would direct. It was re-titled, *Time of My Life*.

◆ ◆ ◆

The writing might have been going well in the autumn of 1990, but other problems occurred which were to coalesce into a major handicap for the show's development.

Having made initial enquiries of Jack Finney, McKenna's agent, Rachel Daniels, needed to formalise the arrangement between the three writers. Keeling was now also represented by Dexter's agent, Mark Hudson, and had moved into Dexter's spare room. Both had become friendly with Hudson on a social as well as a business level.

The problem grew from the fact that McKenna and Daniels had disliked Mark Hudson on sight and Daniels was unimpressed by his business dealings with her. Hudson was taking an active interest in the show. Now it was McKenna's turn to feel that he was being nudged out. He started to resent the time he was spending actually *writing* the piece. Every time he thought he had finished, Dexter would come up with another idea which involved ten or twelve hours more work. McKenna felt that, with Hudson's participation, and his two writing colleagues under the same roof, it was developing into a them and us situation.

A further stumbling block was the definition of Dexter's role in the writing team. At the masterclasses his credit had read, 'Conceived and directed by...' while McKenna was given a full 'Book and Lyrics by...' credit. The question, 'What happens if a producer picks up the show but will not let Dexter direct?' complicated matters further.

Originally, the writers had agreed (quite correctly) on a straightforward three-way split. Now, McKenna felt that with Hudson's influence this would give him no say in how the piece developed - he could never counterbalance a two-thirds majority. The agreement with Finney gave the novelist 25% of the authors' royalties, for the use of the underlying material. This left 75% to be divided between Dexter, Keeling and McKenna. It could logically be divided into 25% for music, 25% for lyrics and 25% for book. Daniels felt that McKenna should receive all the book and lyrics royalties, while Dexter would get his royalties from directing the show. In the end, after some furious arguments, McKenna agreed to 25% for Keeling, 12.5% for Dexter and 37.5% for himself, with the caveat that should Dexter not end up directing the show, this could be revised. Dexter reluctantly conceded, though he felt aggrieved that his contribution was not properly acknowledged.

In McKenna's defence, he felt that if he held a full half-interest in the piece, he could at least prevent what he saw as the Hudson-Dexter-Keeling grouping taking the project in a direction he strongly opposed. It was agreed, and ratified on paper, that all artistic decisions had to be unanimous.

As all these negotiations went on while the rewrites were being undertaken, it was only a shared belief in the show itself which kept the team together.

[My heart sinks as I re-read this. This situation could only ever have ended badly. Here's another bit of hard-earned wisdom. Whatever the arguments about "x amount for music, x for lyrics, x for book," the working relationship is way more valuable than the money (which is notional anyway). If there are two people collaborating, divide the royalties in half. If there are three, divide it three ways. Seriously!]

◆ ◆ ◆

The National Theatre wanted to see a draft script with a demo tape. The writers knew they could get good performers to contribute their work free, but none of them had the money to buy studio time. Hudson stepped into the breach and offered to pay for it (He was subsequently to deduct these studio fees from royalties Dexter and Keeling received for other work). The recording date was set for Sunday November 4th and the demo was cast with Caroline O'Connor as Maddie, Greg Ellis as Nick, Teddy Kempner as Al, Mary Millar as Mrs van Arc and Leigh Macdonald as Sally. Once again, McKenna's examining work for LAMDA prevented him attending, increasing his sense of isolation.

Caroline O'Connor fell ill on Saturday November 3rd and a late night telephone call left Dexter and Keeling panicking. Early on Sunday morning, Hudson called another of his clients, Bonnie Langford, who generously agreed to take over. She came to the studio, worked incredibly hard learning the eight numbers and the tape was completed.

[An incredibly generous act by a woman of whom I have only ever heard lovely things. I was about to make another horrible mistake. SMcK]

At that time, Bonnie had not fully escaped from her moppet child star image, even though she was now an adult performer. She is a fiercely talented performer, with a big singing voice. The demo recording showed this off and did justice to Keeling's score.

Semi-public presentations were planned for the final week of the National Studio workshop. When it came to casting, Dexter was allowed to bring in a few outside performers but would otherwise use National Theatre players. It was clearly important that whoever played Jan/Maddie must be able to sing it. Caroline O'Connor was working and unavailable. The idea of using Bonnie Langford came up. Langford was keen - it was very different from the roles with which she was normally associated and could help to mark a change of image. Hudson was very keen indeed - for the same reasons. Keeling and Dexter had liked Langford and admired her professionalism on the day the demo was recorded. McKenna, though, was adamantly opposed. He felt that she was absolutely wrong for the role, and that this could hurt their chances of the piece being picked up. He referred to the written agreement that all artistic decisions must be unanimous and put an embargo on Bonnie Langford.

It was too late. Under enormous pressure from Hudson, Dexter had already offered her the role and a contract had been signed. Dexter felt that having a well-known name in the workshop would be in the best interests of the show and attract attention to the piece. He hoped to be able to talk McKenna round.

It was not to be. McKenna felt betrayed - his worst fears about being effectively removed from an active role in the development of the show appeared to have come to pass. There was an almighty row, harsh words were exchanged, telephones slammed down - and McKenna walked off the project.

Keeling and Dexter were very distressed and attempted a reconciliation, but McKenna was adamant.

[Oh dear, here I go again, being grand! Always a mistake. SMcK]

Now the National Theatre workshop was in jeopardy, as McKenna withdrew his book and lyrics. Rachel Daniels' calmer wisdom prevailed and, in return for a ratification of the royalty split, agreed to let Dexter and Keeling use McKenna's work at the National 'and subsequently.' 'Subsequently' was never clearly defined, and this would lead to future contractual problems. The negotiations with Jack Finney were also handed over to Hudson.

Ironically, it was shortly after the split that an article appeared in *The Stage* newspaper, talking about the difficulty of getting new musicals produced and harking back to the Oxford presentation. Part of it read:

> Young producers need look no further for a really true musical comedy called *Maxie* by Stephen Keeling and Shaun McKenna (based on the film). The distinguished audience (including Sondheim, Lionel Bart, Peter Nichols and Cameron Mackintosh) hugged themselves with glee at showstopping numbers like *I'll Find Time For You* and one which should be called *Second Chances Don't Often Come Around.*

Dexter and Keeling undertook the National Studio project while McKenna stayed in Brighton and seethed. He had just started working as Principal of Examinations at LAMDA (his attempt at being freelance having left him in penury), and he tried to put all thoughts of *Time of My Life* out of his mind. Enough of a bridge was built, however, that he sent his colleagues a good-luck card.

◆ ◆ ◆

The National workshop took place in May 1991. The cast was headed by Bonnie Langford as Jan/Maddie, with David Malek as Nick, Teddy Kempner as Al, Miriam Cyr as Sally, and Tom Chadbon and Simon Coates playing smaller roles. Dexter directed, Michael Haslem was Musical Director, Matthew Calliste provided the sound and the stage management team consisted of Sarah Newall and Chantal Hauser. Cameron Mackintosh generously provided office space.

There was one embarrassing incident in Mackintosh's offices, which contain a number of cupboard kitchens. Keeling and Langford were working on a song and had set a pot of coffee to brew. However, Keeling had failed to turn a key switch on the machine, which they left merrily bubbling away while they went upstairs to go over the melody line. As Langford was singing, they heard an explosion from downstairs. Rushing down in a panic, they discovered that the coffee machine had exploded, completely destroying the tiny kitchen. Mackintosh generously agreed not to bill them for the damage!

During his preparations for the workshop, and in the absence of McKenna, Dexter began to write scenes and dialogue. This built his confidence enormously and, in rehearsing the show, Dexter discovered and tried to resolve some problems in the existing script. The opening number, *Just This Wall*, did not work. The difficulty vividly illustrated Sondheim's point about letting the audience know early on what kind of show they were going to see. Starting the show with a row between Jan and Nick did not suggest musical comedy.

Another running concern throughout the writing process had been establishing Jan sufficiently clearly that the audience would care about her. Maddie is obviously appealing - gutsy, energetic, optimistic and full of life. Jan is quieter and softer - but is, in fact, the central figure in the story. It is through her experience of being possessed that Jan learns how to live. There was a danger that, in establishing the problems in the marriage, Jan appeared an unsympathetic, whining nag.

Just This Wall was cut during the rehearsal process. Instead, Dexter wrote some dialogue exchanges which were funny but which did not entirely solve the problem. Given that there were not the resources to present the choreographed Prologue, Scene One was rather downbeat. Al's number, *Maddie Dancing*, became the first song in the show and, while beautiful, was melancholy. Scene One also seemed slow, as the story of Maddie's past life had to be told. Not until Scene Two and *Eligible Men* did the comedy kick into action and the audience was a little taken aback by the sudden change.

Swing Me High threw up the question of how much Nick should dance. There was nothing in the story to suggest that he was capable of dancing well, though Maddie would clearly be expert. Rather than go into a big, choreographic routine, it helped the reality of the show if he was a little awkward and uncomfortable.

Towards the end of the rehearsal process, Dexter took the drastic step of replacing the actress playing Mrs van Arc. One of

Mark Hudson's clients, Lorna Dallas, stepped into the breach and sang the role sensationally well.

The presentations to interested parties took place on Tuesday May 14th, Thursday May 16th and Friday May 17th. Dexter was rightly proud of his production and telephoned McKenna to invite him to see one of the performances. McKenna refused to take the call. Instead, his agent, Rachel Daniels, went to the final presentation and was impressed by what Dexter had achieved.

The response to the National workshop from industry insiders was more muted than it had been at Oxford and the Lilian Baylis, but it was still positive. Cameron Mackintosh did not attend but his second-in-command, Nick Allott, saw the show and, in a subsequent telephone call to Hudson, said that he did not feel the show had a future.

However, one producer did. Andrew Fell from Pola Jones saw the final presentation, loved it and picked up an option. Pola Jones had recently produced the phenomenally successful *Return to the Forbidden Planet* by Bob Carlton, and were shortly to be involved in a major tour of Mike Ockrent's long-running West End hit, *Me and My Girl* and an entirely new production of *My Fair Lady*. This was to be directed by Simon Callow, who had recently won an Oliver award for his Old Vic production of *Carmen Jones*.

Keeling's favourite anecdote about the show concerns the evening that Mark Hudson signed the contract with Pola Jones. Hudson, Fell, Dexter and Keeling were at Pola Jones' London flat. The moment Hudson put pen to paper, there was an enormous thunderclap overhead. They all made a joke of it at the time, but it was to prove fateful.

Fell believed the show had the potential to be a hit but needed further work. He set to, with Dexter and Keeling, to produce a new script.

One of the first things to go was the TV commercial number, which Fell found embarrassing as well as illogical. They decided to write a very short piece advertising tomato ketchup (as in the novel). Keeling was playing a newly-composed Charleston when Dexter suddenly said, 'Stop! Slow it down.' Keeling played the melody at half-tempo. Dexter said, 'Lose the left hand.' What emerged was a lyrical, romantic ballad. They played it to Fell, who loved it, and *Easy* was born. It replaced *Swing Me High* as the moment when Nick and Maddie fall in love. Drawing on McKenna's earlier settings for that moment, and adding some inspiration of their own, they devised a lyric.

During the summer of 1991, Fell and Dexter worked very hard on the book. While both were skilled at devising the shape of each scene, neither were able to write dialogue that sprang from the page. As nine months had elapsed since the row, they agreed that Fell should approach McKenna to see just how final his resignation was.

Fell and McKenna met, and McKenna agreed to read the new script and offer comments. Some of his criticism was unduly harsh and personal, but he also brought up some valid points. He was particularly concerned at the lack of an opening number. He wanted to be back on the project but was too proud to say so directly. He wrote a lyric for a proposed new opening argument song, *How In The World,* and submitted it. Keeling set it and Fell arranged a reconciliation dinner at Joe Allen's in November 1991. Dexter and McKenna patched up their quarrel, though it was to be a while before the antagonism finally died between them.

McKenna was back on the team but he felt his position was

equivocal. Dexter and Keeling had purchased the option on the rights to the underlying property. Because McKenna had given permission during the estrangement for his work to be used at the National Theatre and 'subsequently,' he had no control whatever over the project. He could be thrown off it again at any time. However, a new working partnership was established with the three writers and Andrew Fell, with Fell, as the producer, being the final arbiter in any dispute. It seemed to work.

Rewriting *Time of My Life,* at first, was a question of cutting and polishing. The quartet, *Eligible Men,* was rewritten and the song became *All I Want*:

All I want is somebody to love me.
Dear God, here's a girl on bended knees.
All I want's a guy who'll really love me,
So, Father in Heaven, help me please...

Fell was forceful about the difficulty of raising investment for an unknown show by unknown writers (though McKenna had just had his first radio play broadcast and was working on another commission from Northampton). His tack was to find a star to give the show clout - among others, Walter Matthau was approached to play Al and Ann-Margret was targeted as a potential Mrs van Arc. However, Fell's approaches came to nothing, so he decided to try for a big-name director instead.

The first step was to make a new demo tape, as the material had changed radically. Fell hired a studio and called in some favours. John Barrowman, who was then a rising star after his appearances in *Anything Goes* and *Matador*, played Nick and sang superbly. Mary Millar, whom everyone felt was an irreplaceable Mrs van Arc, reprised her role. Teddy Kempner played Al, as he had done at the National and Jacqui Scott, who had toured successfully as Evita, made a wholly credible Jan/Maddie.

Fell unsuccessfully approached a number of big name directors, including Michael Blakemore, Alan Ayckbourn and Trevor Nunn. Ayckbourn liked the script but disliked the music - and also pointed out politely that the title would have to change as his new comedy, shortly to premiere at Scarborough, was also entitled *Time Of My Life.* Simon Callow looked like being a possibility for a while, but the *My Fair Lady* tour did not go well and this caused Fell to change his mind. The writers wonder now whether Callow was actually ever offered the project.

In the spring of 1992, Fell was working a great deal with Mike Ockrent on the tour of *Me and My Girl.* Ockrent's latest show, *Crazy For You*, was a huge hit on Broadway and was expected to arrive in London imminently. Fell thought Ockrent was the ideal director for *Time of My Life* and decided to set about wooing him.

He sent the script and demo tape. Ockrent was positive and polite about the piece but felt it was not for him. Fell would not give up. He hired the Fortune Theatre on May 22nd 1992 and set up a rehearsed reading, which Dexter directed, and to which Ockrent was be brought along. Dexter assembled a team of five top-notch players, headed by Caroline O'Connor, John Barrowman and Mary Millar. Fell did not want the performers to be over-awed by the presence of one of the world's hottest directors, nor feel they had to 'sell' themselves or the show. He told them that the purpose of the reading was to see whether the piece worked. He did not tell them Ockrent was coming - until half an hour before he arrived.

The company were upset and angry at not being told the true purpose of the presentation. Whereas it had been rehearsed sitting in chairs, scripts in hand, the actors now felt the need to pitch the show to the dress circle, where Ockrent was sitting. They were soon on their feet, improvising moves. The actor playing Al was so thrown by the experience that he delivered

Maddie Dancing from a crouched position. It was not until half-way through the first act that the presentation started to catch fire.

Ockrent came down afterwards, met the writers and the cast. He was entirely charming and said many positive things about the show, but was non-committal. He later told Fell that the show was still not for him.

Fell would not give up. He was so determined to get Ockrent onto the project that he called a writers meeting and mooted the suggestion that a more radical re-write be undertaken. Ockrent directed big, spectacular musical comedies. *Time Of My Life* was a small to medium-sized show without many opportunities for spectacle or ensemble work. It was time, Fell declared, to re-conceive it as a large-scale musical comedy that could fill the London Palladium.

Keeling, McKenna and Dexter had serious reservations. However, Fell was the producer and he called the tune. It remained the only chance they had to see *Time Of My Life* on stage. They began to think of ways of expanding the piece.

ENTR'ACTE

The resumption of the working relationship between the three writers was eased by an interesting development. Late in 1991, just as McKenna and Dexter were reconciled, Ed Hardy – one of the participants in the Sondheim masterclasses (who would later go on to write the lyrics to Boublil and Schoenberg's *Martin Guerre)* – was keen to create some kind of musical theatre writer's collective.

Most of the Masterclass participants had found great difficulties in progressing their work beyond the workshop stage. Denise Wharmby had achieved a production of her spoof Gothic show, *Horatorio* in Australia and a Canadian composer, Leslie Arden, had seen her *Harvest Moon Rising* performed in Canada. None of the British participants, though, had so far had any luck whatever.

All felt that it was an indictment of the state of British theatre that nobody was prepared to take a risk on a new musical. Ed Hardy, Keeling and Dexter were invited to a small dinner party given by Kenny Wax at his flat in West Hampstead. Kenny was currently administrator of the tiny but influential King's Head Theatre in Islington, was determined to be a producer in his own right and had been very interested in the material produced by the Sondheim masterclasses. Wax recalls:

> Ed Hardy, who I knew because he's a distant cousin

from Manchester, had approached me while I was working at the King's Head, and had asked if I'd be interested to be an administrator for a new writers' collective. I couldn't see myself doing that – I really wanted to produce and didn't want to get side-tracked – so I said No. A few weeks later, I gave a little dinner party at my flat in West Hampstead with Steven Dexter, Ed Hardy and Stephen Keeling. Round the table, I said I would love to produce a show that everybody could contribute to – "everybody" being the Sondheim masterclass writers and other up and coming musical theatre writers of the time. Two or three ideas were mooted and the one that seemed to be the best was the idea of a Greek legend. Dexter knew the writer and lyricist Stephen Clark who seemed an ideal person to pull everything together.

At that stage, I'd done some Sunday night concerts and wasn't really equipped to do this. Dexter had another producing friend, Sacha Brooks, who might be interested to come on board. I was a bit defensive at first but Sacha was totally invaluable, we couldn't have done it without him and now he's a long term consultant on all of my shows.

Out of this meeting would not only grow a show but a brand new organisation to promote new activity in musical theatre. The Sondheim masterclass participants were to be the core of this organisation, and other young composers and lyricists - McKenna amongst them - were invited to join. Among the new recruits were Howard Goodall, George Stiles, Anthony Drewe, Stephen Clark and Charles Hart, the lyricist for *Aspects of Love* and *Phantom of the Opera*.

Hardy held a party at his Ladbroke Grove flat and in April 1992 the organisation was officially formed. Subsequent meetings were held at Charles Hart's splendid Notting Hill home, the converted Mercury Theatre - the first home of the Ballets Rambert. It was this venue which gave the organisation its name - The Mercury Workshop. Sondheim quickly agreed to be its Patron.

The Mercury's first 'mission statement' read:

> Formed in April 1992 by Edward Hardy and Charles Hart, The Mercury Workshop is a group of songwriters dedicated to the development and presentation of new writing for the musical theatre stage. It functions without any outside funding and is based at The Mercury Theatre in West London. The group will be supporting and developing the work of its members through informal presentations, workshops and eventually full productions.

Now Kenny Wax's idea of a show to which everyone could contribute came to the fore, in order to make the maximum impact and to establish the Mercury Workshop as a real force in modern musical theatre. This would be a collaborative effort between all the Mercury's members - twenty eight of them. Dexter came on board as director and helped to choose the final theme - the legend of Daedalus and Icarus, intertwined with Theseus and the Minotaur.

According to legend, Daedalus was a master-inventor on the island of Crete. His master, King Minos, was married to Queen Pasiphae who failed to pay the goddess Aphrodite the proper respect, In revenge, Aphrodite caused Pasiphae to conceive a desire to make love to a bull. Daedalus's mechanical artistry made this possible, but there was to be a tragic outcome. Pasiphae gave birth to the Minotaur, half-bull and half-man, who was immured in an elaborate maze, designed by Daedalus.

Every year, the powerful Minos demanded tribute of Athens in the form of ten young men and ten young women who were to be fed to the Minotaur. Theseus, Prince of Athens, came to Crete as one of the sacrificial victims. Minos' daughter, Ariadne, fell in love with him and provided him with a ball of thread so that, having once killed the Minotaur, he could escape through the maze. Daedalus helped Theseus and Ariadne to escape and, fearing Minos' retribution, built wings which would aid him and his son, Icarus, to fly from Crete. Famously, Icarus flew too near the sun, the wax holding the wings together melted and the boy plunged to his death. Daedalus took refuge with the King of Sicily but Minos was still bent on revenge. He set a challenge - to thread a cockleshell with a spider web - knowing that Daedalus was the only man in the world capable of solving such a puzzle. When he did so, Minos arrived in Sicily - but was killed when the daughters of the King of Sicily poured pitch into his bath and effectively boiled him alive.

The show would be performed for one night only - at the Shaw Theatre, Euston Road on Sunday July 19th 1992. Kenny Wax and Sacha Brooks would produce.

The Daedalus story was divided into eighteen sections. Composer and lyricist teams were invited to bid for the section they wanted. Kenny Wax recalls:

> There were three or four of us involved in the divvying up of sections. We asked each of the writing teams to choose three sections they'd like to do – and then, collectively knowing the strengths of each team, we decided which would suit people best.

McKenna and Keeling got the section of their choice (aided by Dexter's presence as director) and were faced with tackling the death of the villainous King Minos and the Finale. They set to work and two numbers were quickly produced: *Minos Is Here* and *If I Told You*.

The project, growing as it did from the Sondheim masterclasses, attracted a great deal of press attention. A report by James Dellingpole in *The Daily Telegraph* read, in part:

> Written, rehearsed and staged in the space of three months, the musical... is designed as a showcase for the contributors, not as a commercial venture.
>
> "It's not meant to be a blockbuster musical. It's an experiment. It will probably work in some bits but not in others," says Edward Hardy, joint artistic director of the Mercury Workshop... The project is supported by Sondheim, who helped select four musical motifs for the show. These refrains - consisting of four or five notes lifted at random from composers like Bach and Chopin - will be injected into the piece to give it a sense of musical unity.
>
> ...Hardy says *The Challenge* was inspired partly by the general despair among young musical writers, sick of waiting six years - the usual gap between the time a work is conceived and put on stage - to see their projects developed. As Hardy points out, the only way of developing as a musical composer is to write more shows. But this is difficult when musical theatre is dominated by two composers (Andrew Lloyd Webber and Stephen Sondheim) and one producer (Cameron Mackintosh). Kit Hesketh-Harvey adds that the spate of musical disasters - notably Mackintosh's *Moby Dick* - has not helped. "There's a crisis of confidence. Producers have become over-cautious." He says there is no shortage of investors. "It's not unduly difficult to raise finance. You might as well lose it on Shaftesbury Avenue as at Lloyd's. It's a lot more fun." The biggest problem, says Hesketh-Harvey, is the

> blockbuster musical. He said, "It's becoming a joke. A big media circus with colossal hype and colossal self-interest." The Mercury Workshop's aim is to revive small-scale musical theatre which can survive on its own merits without a two million pound budget.

The journalist Mark Pappenheim came to the meeting at the Mercury Theatre when all the writers presented their completed sections to each other - and Stephen Clark (who was to write the book and give the piece its internal logic) saw the material he would have to unify. Pappenheim wrote an observant piece in *The Independent*:

> Continuity was now Clark's chief concern: by letting each pair of composer-lyricists go off and write their own sections in isolation, small dramatic inconsistencies had inevitably crept in. The variety, even clash, of musical styles between numbers was always meant to be a virtue of the piece, but the integrity of the plot had to be preserved at all costs. There were other discrepancies too.
>
> 'One thing we have to talk about is pronounciation [sic],' announced director Steven Dexter. 'Pro*nun*ciation,' enunciated Hart. Confronted with a cast of largely unfamiliar mythological names, the rhymesters had panicked. Daedalus and Pasiphae proved particularly problematic. Was it 'Dead-alus', 'Die-dalus','Dee-dalus' or even 'Day-dalus'? 'Pacify' or 'Pacifier'? "I thought she had one of those dotty things on her E,' someone ventured bravely...
>
> The jokers too had gone wild. I lost count of the number of 'plus Minos' jokes (geddit?), while Pasiphae's backseat approach to love making offered a clear opening for endless innuendo - topped by Stiles and

Drewe's cud-chewing chorus, 'I want to have a bull inside my china shop, and I'll keep wooing with my mooing till I do.' After much 'taking the bull by the horns' and 'service with a smile' plus an impromtu coffee-break rendering of *Little White Bull* it seemed that every conceivable bull joke had been milked to death.

Understandably, given the speed with which the project had taken shape, some sections had yet to materialise. Paul James and Ben Mason (Section 3: Aphrodite makes Pasiphae fall in love with the bull) explained that they were just back from the Buxton Quest for New Musicals. 'I've written four lines of which I'm inordinately proud,' said Paul. 'No, six! I wrote two more in the car coming down. But this time next week...'

Producer Kenny Wax has hopes of a regional rep production or even a recording. But for Stephen Clark the process has been its own pupose. "Producers traditionally have a problem with the idea of ephemerality," he observes. "For me, even if nothing happens to it after the Shaw, it will still have done its job. There's something attractive about the idea that, even if Spielberg does ring up, we can say 'No.'" "Have I got news for you!" speaks the voice of his producer, "If Spielberg rings up, we're saying, 'Yes!'"

The roster of writers and composers involved in *The Challenge* was: Adele Anderson, Jason Carr, Stephen Clark (who would go on to work extensively with Dexter and write *Made In Sheffield* with Keeling), Brenda Cooper, Patrick Dineen, Anthony Drewe, Howard Goodall, Edward Hardy, Charles Hart, Kit Hesketh-Harvey, Paul James, Stephen Keeling, Guy Kitchenn (with whom McKenna would write *Give A Girl A Break* and a great many songs), Paul Leigh, Martin Lowe (who would be *Maddie*'s first musical director), Andrew MacBean, Ben Mason, James McConnell, Shaun McKenna, Andrew Peggie, Paul Sand, Peter Spafford, Mary Stewart-David, George Stiles, Sarah Travis, Denise Wharmby, Eric Woolfson and Kate Young.

The single performance at the Shaw Theatre on July 19th 1992 was sold out well in advance and *The Challenge* received a rapturous reception from a largely 'in' audience. The highlights were Caroline O'Connor's outrageous performance as Queen Pasiphae and Philip Cox's dignity and inner torment as Daedalus. Kit Hesketh-Harvey and James McConnell's *Loveable* ('No, you don't understand - I love a bull!') and George Stiles and Anthony Drewe's *Bull In A China Shop* were the comic highlights of the evening, while Kate Young and Paul Leigh's *Working With Wood* provided some memorable lyrical moments. McKenna and Keeling's Finale brought an enthusiastic audience to its feet.

[There is video of this number at https://www.youtube.com/watch?v=YUzuPoFvTpw

If I Tell You was a particular favourite of my wife, Jenny, who used it in her therapeutic work as an addiction counsellor. She found it provoked deep discussion and one or two breakthroughs for her clients. When she was diagnosed with leukaemia, she asked for it to be played at her funeral, and it was. SMcK]

There were some appreciative notices: 'Many hands make bright work,' trumpeted the *Evening Standard*, though it called the Finale, to Keeling's chagrin, 'Broadway at its slushiest.' The *Financial Times* said:

> *The Challenge* doesn't relieve my gloom about the state of the musical because, like the rest of them, it just isn't *musical* enough. Still, in every way it already surpasses dozens of musicals professionally produced in recent years on either side of the Atlantic.

◆ ◆ ◆

While the establishment of The Mercury Workshop and the production of *The Challenge* caused a splash, it was not to make life a great deal easier for the Sondheim masterclass participants - it certainly did not hasten the production of any of their shows. The following year, a second collaborative musical, *The Ten Commandments*, was markedly less successful - though the Mercury was able to fund workshop presentations of some interesting new work. They also presented a well-received *Mercury Workshop Musical Revue* at the Jermyn Street Theatre in 1994.

Initially under the guidance of Ed Hardy and subsequently with Jenny Bennett and Anton Agalbato at the helm, The Mercury has attracted funding and some star names - Cameron Mackintosh became a Patron and, after directing the 1994 revue, Julia McKenzie took on the role of President. At the time of writing, there are interesting schools initiatives and an expanded Musical Theatre Writing Development programme, including a tie-in with the Royal National Theatre Studio.

[The Mercury Workshop subsequently changed its name to Mercury Musical Developments and more information can be found at www.mercurymusicals.com. SMcK]

I'VE ALWAYS KNOWN

...And do I want
To start again?

In the autumn of 1992, their working relationship revitalised after the experience of *The Challenge*, the three writers, under Andrew Fell's direction, set about turning *Time Of My Life* into a large-scale musical. After some initial meetings, where all manner of ideas were discussed, the four agreed that they needed a period of concentrated, intensive work on the show.

P.S. I can't tell you how pleased I am to be friends again. Lets never do that again!

They all cleared the week of September 28th and agreed to meet daily at Dexter's flat. Dexter and McKenna now had much more respect for each other's work - both had progressed in their careers and it is fair to say that neither man was as defensive about his own contributions as in earlier days. The needs of the show came above the needs of their egos.

The first radical revision was to shift the location of the story from San Francisco to Los Angeles. This meant that the whole society was focussed on the film world.

The Prologue now came into its own and established the style and size of the show. It became a number called *In Hollywood.*

The action begins with Hugo Dahl, the film producer, testing actresses for his new movie. He is unable to find the star he needs:

Someone out there is perfection.
Haven't located her yet.
Think in a different direction.
We'll have to widen the net.

The number travels through the studio, ending with a crowd of hopefuls outside the gates, singing the praises of Hollywood:

We stare at the screen
And we know it's a game,
That they're playing a scene -
We believe, all the same
'Cos our favourite town
Never lets us down -
It's Hollywood.
There is never a doubt
That the problems will heal
'Cos it always works out
In the very last reel.
We all count on you!
Make our dreams come true
In Hollywood!

A gauze drops in, onto which is projected a flickering black and white image. Nick is looking through Al's collection of old silent movies. Nick is now a film editor, recently re-located to LA and staying with his grandfather while they find a suitable house. Nick is very taken with footage he discovers, which Al reveals to be Maddie Marsh. He sings *Maddie, Dancing.* Abe van Arc was directing Maddie in *Daughters of Jazz* when her car hit a tree, but rumour has it that he cut her footage into his own private copy of the movie. Van Arc has recently died and there is to be a huge charity auction of his unique film collection in a few days time. Al encourages Nick to 'visit the widow, and flirt. It's how business is done in this town.'

The action moves to Mrs van Arc's house, where she is established in a number with an adoring chorus.
The first version of this was called *Goodbye Louis* (her late husband, Abe van Arc, being renamed Louis van Arc) but this was felt to be too 1920s in style. A replacement number was written for Mrs van Arc and her caterers, in which she explains her philosophy of life:

My whole married life
Was a miserable joke
Till a week ago last Friday
When I watched the bastard croak.
The funeral I planned
With meticulous care...
These social obligations
Must be carried off with flair.
Never leave a detail to chance.
Watch your reputation advance.

Nick visits her to ask to see *Daughters of Jazz.* Mrs van Arc lends it to him and invites him to the auction. The gauze flies back in, onto which is projected the film of Maddie's car crash.

The action then continues largely as before. In the party scene, there is a big ensemble number called *The Schmooze*, for which

Keeling wrote a clever, cyclical structure and McKenna wrote a sharp lyric in which half a dozen individual characters were identified and followed. The tone was cynical - indeed, Fell made McKenna watch Robert Altman's film *The Player* twice before attempting to write the lyric.

Fell believed that *I'll Find Time For You* (which had stopped the show in Oxford and London) was not suitable as a party song and instructed McKenna and Keeling to come up with something in the style of Cole Porter ('but better!'). What emerged was *Time After Time*, a title also being considered for the show itself:

If you want to please me
Don't stand there and tease me -
Here is what will make this baby's day.

The simplest of things
That nature can muster -
A nightgown that clings,
A cute diamond cluster...
When baby's remote
You know what'll please her -
A tigerskin coat
And a Hispano Suiza.
Lavish these gifts
On a girl in her prime.
They'll make her happy
Time after time...

The song took a more sexual turn in the final chorus, aimed directly at Nick:

That masculine stance,
Your talent for wooing.
One smouldering glance

Could be my undoing.
I'm ready to listen
To all you suggest.
You seize your chance
And let me do the rest.
The tip of the tongue,
A strap off the shoulder...
We're ready, we're young!
Let's try something bolder...

It was clear by this time that the team were working well together and that the new material was sharp. Keeling produced some memorable tunes and McKenna's lyrics were obeying Sondheim's rules. Dexter and McKenna were working creatively together on the book, in association with Fell. It felt as though everything was going well - yet the writers, in their hearts, were not convinced that what they were doing was right.

After the party scene, the action remained identical until the end of the act. Instead of going to Sally's apartment, Jan went to the bus station where *Never Gonna Speak To Him Again* became an ensemble number - the ensemble including a couple of nuns, a down and out, a student and a hippy. The action of this scene was later transferred to the outside of Grauman's famous Chinese Cinema in Hollywood, where the nuns, etc, became tourists.

Act Two opened with the weakest of the new numbers, *Have You Seen My Wife?*. This was set outside the cinema and was essentially a chase sequence - Nick asking the passers-by where Jan had gone. The remainder of Act Two was essentially the same, with a few interpolations. Keeling was working on another show for which he had only set one lyric. It was a beautiful tune and Fell insisted that, as he had not yet submitted it to the other lyricist, it be incorporated into the *Time Of My Life* score. Keeling reluctantly agreed. It became Jan's introspective ballad, *I've*

Always Known, when she makes the decision to allow Maddie to use her body for the commercial:

I've always known there had to be more.
A life I've never dared to explore.
I built walls to stop my panic showing,
Swore I knew where I was going
When I had no way of knowing.

An ensemble number was added as Dahl and Maddie (in Mrs van Arc's body) enter the studio in Hollywood. Describing the qualities needed in the star they are looking for, Dahl and the ensemble sing:

It's the biggest thing since Selznick
Had to search for Rhett and Scarlett.
We need someone new and different
Who can act like Meryl Streep.
She needs bones like Greta Garbo,
She needs legs like Betty Grable,
She needs balls like Barbara Stanwyck
And we need to get her cheap.
She must have a voice like Streisand,
Be as sweet as Doris Day
And as tough as Bette Davis
In a sexy sort of way.

She must be everything you want in a woman,
She must be everything that touches your heart.
She must be vulnerable, gutsy and funny,
She must be tender, independent and smart.
She must be powerful but not overbearing,
Sensual, discerning and cool,
Practical alluring and daring,
Up to date and nobody's fool.
She must be everything you want in a woman,
She must be everything a man can respect.

She must be somebody you want to accept you
And still be somebody you long to protect.

It was essentially a 'list' number but it was witty and had a very catchy melody. Fell's assistant, Sally, considered it deeply sexist and found it offensive, but the men overrode her objections (which probably proves her point!)

[Looking at it in 2020, I can't believe we ever thought it wasn't sexist. In my defence, when I wrote it I just thought about my wife, as I did when I wrote Afraid. *O tempora, o mores! SMcK]*

◆ ◆ ◆

Not all the work could be done in the one intensive week. McKenna found himself writing till midnight every night, and all weekend, during October and November 1992. Fell took a very active interest in every detail of the draft - down to the commas in the stage directions. Fell even spoke to Keeling on his mobile phone from the Oxford hospital while his wife was giving birth to their third child in the next room!

McKenna recalls a telephone conversation with Fell while the producer was driving home up the M40. Fell had just received a tape of *The Schmooze* from Keeling, which McKenna had not yet heard. Fell insisted on playing it on his car stereo while holding his mobile phone to the speakers. McKenna could only gain a vague idea of the song from what he heard, but was suitably enthusiastic. Suddenly there was an almighty bang and Fell muttered, 'Have to call you back. Somebody has just crashed into the back of my car!'

The new songs were recorded by Lorna Dallas as Mrs van Arc, Hal Fowler as Nick and a tremendous group of soloists whom Andrew persuaded to work as an ensemble, including Denise Wharmby (who had been the first-ever Maxie) and Helen Hobson, who had just finished playing Eliza in Pola Jones' *My Fair Lady* and was to go on to star with Cliff Richard in *Heathcliff*.

The new material was sent off to Ockrent. There was no reply for weeks.

Another contractual complication arose when Fell was visiting New York. He took the opportunity to visit Don Congdon, Jack Finney's agent. Here it transpired that Mark Hudson had sold on to Pola Jones certain rights (including merchandising) which he had no right to sell, having never obtained them in the first place.

Fell was furious and threatened litigation. It was some weeks before the situation was sorted out and everybody was happy. McKenna felt that his earlier reluctance to deal with Hudson was vindicated, but even he was astonished when, in the summer of 1993, Hudson suddenly disappeared. The subsequent case made headlines in *The Stage* for several weeks. Hudson had defrauded his clients of a substantial amount of money and the scam was only discovered when his agency amalgamated with a much larger concern. Hudson was told to leave his office and not to contact any of his clients. He did attempt to speak to Keeling, but Keeling declined to accept the call. Hudson was eventually located and charges were pressed. The case went to trial and Hudson was jailed for several months. He is now believed to be a sports therapist in Stoke-on-Trent.

[That's what I was told at the time. But it sounds bitchy and it may just be malicious gossip. Should you ever read this, Mr Hudson, I apologise if I have maligned you. And of course there is nothing wrong with being a sports therapist in Stoke-on-Trent. SMcK]

There was still no word from Ockrent. The writers began to be suspicious that there was a problem when Fell asked for yet more changes to the script. The Prologue remained *In Hollywood*, but this was now set in 1926 and told Maddie's story. It ended with her writing her message on the wall and dancing around the flat in her excitement, whereupon she lost her balance and fell out of the window, killing herself in the process.

[Hmmm... Desperate, or what? SMcK]

Nick became an architect who was to remodel Mrs van Arc's house. *Maddie, Dancing* was cut and a trio for Nick, Jan and Al was written called *Living With...*, about the difficulties of sharing one's home with someone else. *[No trace of this remains. SMcK]*

Attention to Detail was cut and the split-stage quartet returned in a new incarnation, *Total Satisfaction. [Nor of this. SMcK]*

At this point, the three writers felt that all they were doing was re-writing endlessly, with no end in sight. Eventually, McKenna put his foot down and said he would not make any more changes until a director was on board and a production in view.

Because there was no contractual obligation to include McKenna, Fell simply dropped him. However, there had been a glimmer of interest from Mike Ockrent who said he might consider directing the show if it was re-conceived and had a new book writer. Ockrent, Fell, Dexter and Keeling met at Ockrent's London flat.

Maddie's story had always begun when she was dancing at the Alcazar Theatre in a dance troupe called the Blue Belles. The other members of the team were called Trixie, Lilian and Bea. Ockrent thought that if one ghost was funny, four would be even funnier. They came up with a scenario, which Keeling and

Dexter were sent away to develop, in which Maddie died when she accidentally blew up the Alcazar Theatre. Trixie, Lilian and Bea were killed in the same explosion and had spent eternity resenting Maddie. When Maddie possessed Jan, the other three found a way to follow her into the present day and set out to get their revenge.

Once again, Dexter was concerned that *Time Of My Life* seemed to be turning a show a million miles removed from the piece the team had set out to write. The prospect of a lavish production directed by Mike Ockrent was tempting and would be too good an opportunity to turn down - but where was the 'little show with heart' that had wowed the audience at Oxford?

At the time, Dexter was working on *Made In Sheffield*, a new musical with Keeling and Stephen Clark, which had been commissioned by Eileen Fawcett in Sheffield. He also had other directing opportunities, including a production of *Sullivan and Gilbert* by Ken Ludwig. Ludwig had written *Lend Me A Tenor* and the new book to Ockrent's *Crazy For You*. Ludwig seemed to be the ideal choice to approach as a replacement bookwriter for *Time Of My Life*.

Dexter had a meeting scheduled with Ludwig to discuss *Sullivan and Gilbert.* He took the opportunity to bike over to him a copy of the *Time Of My Life* script. Dexter credits Ludwig for putting his finger on exactly what was wrong with the show and the source of Dexter's unease. Ludwig asked him why they were trying to turn a small show about four people into a large-scale Broadway style extravaganza.

The clear-sighted truth of this comment immediately struck home. Dexter returned to Fell and told him that he wanted to return to something closer to the National Theatre version, which had attracted Fell's interest in the first place. Ockrent gave a final 'No' to *Time Of My Life.* Fell brought in Anthony

Drewe, bookwriter and lyricist of *Just So [and, of course, many subsequent hits, including* Betty Blue Eyes, Mary Poppins *and* Half A Sixpence. *SMcK].*

Drewe drafted a new first act in which the subplot concerned Jan's mother, but nobody could get enthusiastic about it. The project seemed dead in the water. Though Fell was to maintain his option for another year, until the summer of 1994, there was no further work on the show and the three writers had to admit that Maddie had finally expired.

It was a classic example of a show losing its way, trying to become something that it was simply not cut out to be. There were sound commercial reasons for the changes - and even some artistic justifications - but they were simply wrong choices. If Fell wanted a large-scale, spectacular musical, he should have started with a different project. The writers all felt that they had been tempted along a wrong path by the twin carrots of fame and fortune.

Time Of My Life had, by this point, been around for so long that word in the business was, basically, 'If it hasn't happened yet, there must be something seriously wrong with it.' The writers knew that they would be unlikely to find another producer. They felt that two and a half years of very hard work had been wasted.

For the next eighteen months, through the second half of 1993 and almost all of 1994, the three writers went their separate ways.

Dexter's directing career took off, with work in London, *Little Shop of Horrors* in Singapore, reworking Cameron Mackintosh's *Moby Dick* in Germany and mounting the premiere of the Stiles-Drewe *Ugly Duckling* at New York.

Keeling began work with Ed Hardy on *The Amazing Mr Blunden* and wrote incidental music for Jonathan Church's production of *The Broken Heart* at the Lyric, Hammersmith.

McKenna continued to run LAMDA Examinations and wrote a radio play about an incident in the life of Jack London, a stage adaptation of *To Serve Them All My Days* for Northampton, and an original thriller, *Ruling Passions*, which was premiered at Northampton and picked up by a West End producer. He also worked with composer Guy Kitchenn on *Give A Girl A Break*, two linked one-act musicals.

There was talk of Dexter, Keeling and McKenna coming together to write something else but the *Time of My Life* experience had ended so negatively, that the impetus was simply not there.

The project was dead. In the story of the show, Maddie Marsh is dead but she refuses to accept it. For the writers, Maddie had become a real person. It may seem fanciful to suggest, but it was almost as though Maddie was determined to have her chance at becoming a star. The next twist in the story came when one of the producers of *The Challenge*, Kenny Wax, picked up the phone and spoke to Steven Dexter.

Maddie was about to come back to life.

IF NOT FOR ME

If not for me
Would there have been
this chance to pull through?

It was not Kenny Wax's lifetime ambition to become a theatre producer. While taking his business studies degree, he spent a year on an industrial placement at Dixons. On graduating, he knew he did not want to spend his life as a personnel manager training staff to sell cameras.

Like the three writers, he had always loved musicals. He was particularly struck when he saw the original production of *Me and My Girl* at the Adelphi, with Robert Lindsay and Emma Thompson. He found it inspiring, making so many people so happy, that he thought he would enjoy being responsible for putting together something that touched such a wide range of lives. From that moment on, he knew what he wanted to do - it then became a question of ensuring that he succeeded.

In his first few months after graduating, Wax worked as a front of house usher on *Miss Saigon*. The show was just opening and impresario Cameron Mackintosh was in and out of the theatre on an almost daily basis. One day, self-conscious in his usher's blue jacket with black lapels, Wax plucked up the courage to hand Mackintosh a letter, the gist of which was, 'Dear Mr Mackintosh, I want to be a producer of musicals just like you. How do I go about it?' Rather than tearing it up, Mackintosh recognised Wax's serious intent and generously invited him to come to his office for a chat.

Mackintosh gave him two pieces of advice which Wax has kept with him to this day. The first was only ever to produce a show that he was passionate about. The second was that, if he was serious about going into producing, Wax would need to learn about every aspect of the industry the hard way - by doing all the jobs!

Wax then joined DeWynters, the West End's leading theatre advertising company, as a runner. This was another humble job for a recent graduate, delivering artwork around the West End, but it was, at least, a connection. Wax not only learned his way around the West End, but also found out about DeWynters' clients and what they were up to. Eventually DeWynters advertised for a permanent position as a media assistant. They received more than a hundred applications but, because Wax was already working for the company, they interviewed him. He won the job. He was finally in the loop.

Wax heard about the Sondheim masterclasses, and the readings and special evenings which had been organised to back up the workshops. He went to the London presentation at the Lilian Baylis Theatre, in July 1990. Here he fell in love with *Maxie.* He was hugely impressed by the star performance of Caroline O'Connor, as well as the piece itself. He was clear that this was the show he wanted to do. However, he was 22, had no experience whatever of producing and did not approach the writers because he did not believe that they would let him anywhere near the piece. He was right. At the time, the lure of a Newbury production was beckoning.

After a year, Wax was looking to gain production experience. He pestered Cameron Mackintosh into giving him a job as a runner on the George Stiles-Anthony Drewe *Just So*, which was about to go into production at the Kilburn Tricycle Theatre. At the first night, Wax met Sue Uings, theatre manager of the New London Theatre, who found him a position on the stage crew of *Cats*.

With a long-running show, there is often a certain apathy among the staff but Wax could not believe that he was working backstage in the West End. Wishing to learn more (and learn it quickly), he started to work in the box office during the day as well as working on the crew at night. Uings generously allowed Wax to further his learning as a follow-spot operator and in the flies.

After a year at *Cats*, he moved on again - this time to his first management position as administrator of the well-known King's Head Theatre in Islington. Here, Wax produced his first shows - a season of Sunday night cabarets. The buzz he felt from these achievements convinced him that he was in the right profession.

His next show was *The Challenge*, discussed in Chapter Five. In the audience at *The Challenge*'s single performance at the Shaw was Gary Withers, the head of the hugely-successful design company, Imagination. Withers was impressed with Wax's achievement, at the relatively tender age of 26, and offered him a job in Imagination's newly-formed theatre division.

Wax invited Dexter, McKenna and Keeling to the lavish launch party of Imagination's theatre division, as he was still interested in acquiring the rights to *Maxie*, should things not work out with Pola Jones.

For Imagination, Wax acquired the rights to, and produced, the Olivier award-winning *Once On This Island*, a Caribbean musical for which the Royalty Theatre was refurbished and re-named the Island Theatre. One of the features of that production, which attracted excellent notices but disappointing audiences, was that the party continued every night in the stalls bar after the show itself had finished.

Wax thoroughly enjoyed his time at Imagination and learned a great deal from it. He felt, though, that the premature closing of *Once On This Island* made it unlikely that the company would embark on a similar project for at least a year. He felt that the time had come to make rather a big decision - to leave Imagination and to try producing a show on his own.

The show Wax wanted to produce was *Maxie*. At this point, Pola Jones still technically had an option on the project but nothing was happening. Wax approached the writers and was very up-front and honest. He said that he could not promise anything, that it would be hard work raising the money - there could be no guarantees. He said that he felt that by now the writers knew him well enough to take a gamble.

They did, though McKenna was by now sceptical, sick of all the false starts. He was happy for Wax to take an option, once the Pola Jones contract lapsed, but he really did not want to be involved in another hectic round of re-writes without a clear end in view.

One of Wax's great supporters during this period was John Cohen, the well-known showbusiness lawyer at Clinton's. Wax approached Cohen when he was leaving Imagination, to handle the legal aspects of *Maddie*. Wax had been characteristically honest - he knew he could not afford the kind of legal fees that a lawyer in Cohen's position would charge. However, the pair came to an understanding and an enormous amount of legal work was done, including the writers' contracts and that with Jack Finney for the underlying material.

Don Congdon, Finney's agent, had become bored with all the problems with the option agreement that had resulted from the involvement with Andrew Fell and Mark Hudson. The original option agreement had now lapsed. Clearly, without such an agreement in place, *Maddie* was dead in the water.

Congdon had reached the point where he was unwilling even to answer correspondence. However, Cohen was visiting New York on other business and managed to make an appointment. They had a very productive meeting and within a fortnight a new contract was signed with Finney.

When the signed contract came through, Cohen commented to Wax on the faintness and frailty of Finney's signature. Three days later, Finney's obituary appeared in the *Daily Telegraph*. Had he not signed the contract when he did, *Maddie* would never have happened. It seemed another of Maddie's twists of fate.

Wax finalised his option in January 1995. He telephoned Keeling, who dropped around a copy of the current script and demo tape. Wax was excited and sat down to read what the writers had been up to since the presentation at the Lilian Bayliss.

He was horrified. It was now a large-scale elaborate show with dancing waiters. He listened to the tape again and again. Finally, he said to Keeling, 'If this is how the show is, I'm no longer interested.' He felt the piece had lost all the charm and intimacy it had had at the workshop. He called a meeting with Dexter and Keeling. He said that he understood why the writers had gone down the path they had, incorporating the ideas of Fell and Ockrent, but that it was absolutely wrong for the piece. This was not the version he wanted to produce. Fortunately, both Dexter and Keeling agreed that they had lost the wood for the trees. They decided to revert to the post-National Theatre version, with one or two changes. Wax thought that Al being Nick's grandfather was rather sentimental, and the character became simply their landlord. He also became rather more grouchy and volatile. *I've Always Known*, Jan's Act Two ballad, was the only new song to be retained from the large-scale version.

Wax was adamant that there needed to be a big Act One number for Mrs van Arc. He telephoned McKenna and gave him a brief for a jazzy, up-tempo, very funny solo number. McKenna demurred, his belief that the show would ever come to anything still profoundly dented. Wax said that he would prefer it if McKenna would write the number, but if not, he would go elsewhere. He had already had a conversation with Anthony Drewe, whose lyrics were always witty and polished. McKenna agreed to draft a lyric but ended up still believing that Scene Two should be a quartet. He therefore submitted a quartet called *Beautiful Things*. This was his fifth song for that slot, so inspiration and enthusiasm were wearing thin. Drewe subsequently came up with a lyric, *Nick-Nacks*, which fulfilled Wax's brief. *Nick Nacks* went into the show.

[I never liked it much but it's perfectly possible that that's just sour grapes. I'm a big fan of Anthony's work. He's a deft and clever wordsmith. It turns out that we both went to the same school, Maidstone Grammar, and though Anthony is younger we were there at the same time. We both had the same inspirational teacher, Donald Scott. SMcK]

◆ ◆ ◆

Having secured an agreement that he could proceed, Wax jumped in with both feet. He gave up his comfortable salary and company car and gave in his notice at Imagination. He felt very sad doing this, as he had enjoyed his work there, and Gary Withers had been very supportive. Wax gave Imagination the opportunity to take *Maddie* on, but so soon after *Once On This Island*, they were reluctant to take such a risk. Gary Withers fully understood and supported Wax's decision to move on and the parting was very amicable.

When he told his parents of his decision, and that he was going to try to raise more than a quarter of a million pounds, they asked him where on earth he thought he could raise that kind of money. He said, in all honesty, 'I don't know.' He believed he could raise the first seventy thousand from people he knew, and was confident that the last tranche of money would come in quickly once the balance was raised, but he had no idea where the crucial middle tranche would come from. However, he told his parents, 'If I don't try, I'll never know.'

Wax's big challenge was, 'How do I do this?' He knew how shows were produced, of course, but he was concerned to find the best route from having a script and a tape to presenting *Maddie* (the agreed new title) on the West End stage. This was a crucial set of choices. Getting any of these wrong could amount to the show failing to achieve its full potential.

Should he go for a small London venue, such as the King's Head, the Soho Laundry, the Arts Theatre, the Lyric Hammersmith Studio or the Tricycle Theatre, Kilburn? This would attract the national critics and would certainly be the most open to the industry. A lot of people would probably see it.

The alternative was to go to a rep outside London and find a theatre where the production values could be of a scale which, with a little imagination, could conceivably transfer to the West End.

Wax felt that the first option was dangerous. Commonly, people in the industry do not have the imagination to see how a show can grow. They see a fringe show and subsequently always think of it as a fringe show. Some shows, like *A Slice of Saturday Night*, can find their proper home in a smaller venue. *A Slice* was a huge hit at the intimate Arts Theatre but was rather lost in the much larger Strand Theatre when it transferred. It had to become a size which it should not have been and, consequently, did not run. *Maddie* had already gone through one experience of over-inflation and Wax was determined not to allow this to happen again. However, even the National Theatre version of *Maddie* was a medium-sized show, and would not sit entirely happily in one of these small London venues.

Wax decided to go the repertory route. He and Keeling set off to perform presentations to a number of regional theatres, including Birmingham Rep and the Yvonne Arnaud Theatre in Guildford.

◆ ◆ ◆

This, in early 1995, was another extraordinary experience for Keeling. He sat at the piano, playing the score and singing the songs, while Wax sold the story of the show with vitality and animation. Wax felt as though the pair of them were baring their souls. Sometimes, they took a singer with them, to play Maddie. Keeling says, 'I don't think people could quite believe it - it was very summer stock/Mickey Rooney time. Some enjoyed it, but others were expecting a full-blown semi-performance. They were completely taken aback! One producer is known to have called us, "a pair of complete arseholes."'

Wax felt as though he was back in the Tin Pan Alley days of the 1920s and 30s. This was exactly how old-time producers and songwriters sold their work and, like those old-timers, Keeling and Wax were kicked in the teeth more than once.

The Birmingham Rep felt that it was not for them. Jamie Barber at Guildford was interested, on the proviso that Wax could get a certain level of star casting - good television names. Wax made enquiries and sent scripts to people who he felt might fit the bill. Unfortunately, whenever he went back to Jamie Barber to suggest So-and-so, the response was, 'So-and-so will be OK as part of a package but isn't a sufficient name by himself.'

This was a frustrating period. Wax always felt that he could get a good level of casting, but that the huge musical names were unlikely to take a risk on a new show by new writers, with a young producer. Wax felt that he could not hold out for Guildford for ever, gathering a suitable company who would be appropriate names for the marquee but not necessarily be the right people for the roles. Instead, he decided to look for a theatre which would be enthusiastic about the show itself, where he could put together the very best cast he could. He always felt confident enough in the show, and about his own ability to cast, to know that he would manage to get excellent performers, even if they were not huge names.

Apart from finding a theatre, Wax also had to raise the money. He went to people he knew and pressed them for seed money. He then arranged a backers presentation in Manchester, at a golf club with which his parents' friends were familiar. Dexter rehearsed a presentation, a slightly extended version of the Oxford and Lilian Bayliss presentations, and assembled a cast including Nicola Dawn (fresh from *Copacabana*) as Maddie, Russell Wilcox as Nick, Philip Cox as Al and Nadia Strahan as Mrs van Arc with Stephen Aintree to narrate. They hired a bus and on Sunday October 1st 1995 the *Maddie* Roadshow hit Manchester.

They brought the house down. People stood and cheered. Wax's belief in the show seemed entirely validated by two hundred members of the general public. The entire team left Manchester on a high.

Unfortunately, in the succeeding weeks, that enthusiasm was not converted into investment - at least, not on a large scale. Wax was disappointed with the response. He decided to repeat the process in London.

For the London presentation, Wax was delighted to obtain the services of Patrick Cargill as Al. Cargill agreed to participate on the basis that he would be given first refusal of the role in any subsequent production, and he was certainly a name that Guildford were happy with. The remainder of the company remained as before.

With something finally happening, McKenna decided that there really was a chance that *Maddie* had a future and came back onto the project. He was never to detach himself from it again. He and Dexter developed an easy new working relationship in which they were genuinely collaborating on the book. One would draft a scene and fax it to the other. He would amend it and fax it back. After three or four fax transmissions and some lengthy phone calls, both writers were happy.

The London showcases were booked into the intimate Players Theatre, under the arches at Charing Cross and home to music hall. *[Now the Charing Cross Theatre and, at the time of writing, a home for revivals and UK premieres of smaller-scale musicals. SMcK]* The Players is a tiny gem of a theatre, the ambience warm and comfortable. Using the stage, and the resident star-cloth, everyone was confident that it was a perfect venue for the *Maddie* showcase. Two performances were scheduled on November 6th, the first at 5.30pm as this would suit the end of the working day for the key industry people Wax was hoping to attract. The second performance was at 8pm.

Kenneth Wax
presents a showcase for

MADDIE

Music By Stephen Keeling

Book & Lyrics by Shaun McKenna
and Steven Dexter

Directed by Steven Dexter

Based on a novel "Marion's Wall"
by Jack Finney

Todays showcase is kindly sponsored by
Levy Gee Chartered Accountants

The showcases did not repeat the Manchester success. At the early performance, to which a great many influential people were invited, it simply did not click. The songs were received with polite applause, the jokes in desperate silence. Most of them had seen this presentation two or three times before. Keeling was at the piano, eagerly trying to inject as much animation into the performance as possible. The actors were working hard, and as the showcase progressed, started to work a little too hard. McKenna's heart sank further and further into his boots. Andrew Fell arrived and smiled knowingly at the writers afterwards.

The evening show went better but still did not sparkle. The writers were deeply depressed. They all felt that this was probably the end of the road for *Maddie*, that the new dawn they had seen with Wax's enthusiasm and energy was in danger of petering out. The sole mitigating factor for McKenna was the opportunity to meet Lionel Bart.

However, to everyone's surprise, the money that Wax managed to raise from a combination of the London and Manchester audiences was sufficient to enable him to commit to a co-producing deal with a repertory theatre. Bloody but unbowed, the team forged ahead.

◆ ◆ ◆

Martin Connor was Wax's choice as director. Connor is an actor/director whose London credits include the West End run of *Wonderful Town* with Maureen Lipman and West End revivals of *Stepping Out, You Can't Take It With You* and *Rough Crossing.*

Connor knew Wax through Dan Crawford, Artistic Director of the King's Head Theatre in Islington. Crawford had been responsible for mounting *Wonderful Town* at the Queens Theatre after seeing Connor's production of it with students at the Guildhall School of Music and Drama.

Wax invited Connor to Imagination where he and Keeling did one of their 'Tin Pan Alley' presentations. Connor was impressed by a 'quality of joy' which seemed to come from the script – and by Wax's enthusiasm for it. Connor's gut reaction was that *Maddie* was a good yarn, well-crafted, with honesty and truth at the centre of it and very good tunes. One of the things which attracted him to the show was a certain sense of spirituality, as yet unfocussed, which he felt was a rare and unusual quality in a modern musical.

Wax felt that Dexter was more than capable of directing the show effectively, but that he was too close to it to bring an objective eye to the proceedings. Dexter's experience of directing the presentations bore out Wax's gut reaction. Dexter had directed these scenes five or six times, by now, and felt he was using staging which he knew worked, rather than coming fresh to the show with a clear vision. He, too, was happy with the appointment of Connor. He had been impressed by *Wonderful Town* and had, indeed, recommended Connor to producer Ronnie Lee to direct a Japanese tour of Rodgers and Hammerstein's *Cinderella*.

The next addition to the team was the distinguished choreographer, David Toguri. Toguri won an Olivier award for the National Theatre's *Guys and Dolls* and was Olivier-nominated in two categories for Wax's production of *Once On This Island*. His other credits included, in the West End, *The Blue Angel, Spread A Little Happiness, Jumpers, Swell Party, The Baker's Wife* and *Noel and Gertie*. One of Toguri's specialities is choreography for actors, rather than dancers. He was to be in charge of 'musical staging' on *Maddie*. He and Connor had worked together frequently since they first met on *Wonderful Town*.

Connor says of Toguri:

> I remember directing a student production at Guild-

> hall which David staged. I like working with students because of their energy. David was far from well at the time but I remember him in the rehearsal room. He had more joy, energy and delight than all those young students put together.

The writers were heartened that Wax had managed to get such good people in key roles, and they all met up in December 1995 at Wax's flat to discuss the script.

Dexter had already done some work before McKenna's return and now it was largely a case of polishing. Connor came up with some key points. Maddie now meets her death in 1926 because she takes Al's car and is an inexperienced driver - in other words, she dies because of her own character, not some random act of fate. *How In The World*, with an adjusted lyric, was reinstated in order to establish the tension in the marriage. Because Jan runs off to Sally towards the end of Act One, and the Scene Two quartet was replaced by *Nick Nacks*, Sally had to be introduced briefly in the opening scene, giving rise to some potential comedy.

Connor expressed the concern that there were no ensemble numbers in the show. McKenna and Dexter were quite keen to revive *Everything You Want In A Woman*, a notion which did not appeal to Wax.

Connor's overriding point at these discussions was that the piece was workmanlike and clear but it rambled in places and lacked focus, fun and wit. He also felt that the spiritual elements could be explored more fully. He discovered in these discussions that there had been more wit in earlier drafts but that it had somehow faded away during the rewriting process.

Dexter and McKenna set about the re-writes, which were quickly achieved. Connor was surprised and impressed by the changes they made. He had thought that the piece might need two or three further drafts before all his concerns were fully addressed. Now, reading the new, tightened draft, he felt that this was a script he would be happy to take into rehearsal. It was at this point that Connor felt absolutely confident that he would enjoy working with these people, on this project.

Keeling was now faced with writing out the entire score, including the musical underscoring for key scenes. He had never done this before - in the various presentations, he had always played from memory. It took him three months.

◆ ◆ ◆

Keeling and Dexter had worked with a young director named Jonathan Church at the Sheffield Crucible on their production of *Made In Sheffield.* Church had just taken over as Artistic Director of the Salisbury Playhouse.

[Jonathan Church has subsequently been Artistic Director of the Birmingham Rep Theatre, Chichester Festival Theatre and Sydney Theatre Company. At the helm of Jonathan Church Productions, he is responsible for many successful West End shows. SMcK]

Dexter and Keeling suggested that Wax speak to Church, as he was the youngest artistic director in the UK. This attracted the young producer's interest.

Wax sent a script and a tape. Because Church saw names he knew on the cover, it was not 'consigned to the pile' but read quickly. Church had collaborated with Keeling on *The Broken Heart* at the Lyric Hammersmith Studio and was a great admirer of his music. 'I was very excited by Keeling's work and by the quality of music he could come up with almost on the hoof.' The tape immediately struck Church as working well, and he liked the script. He was attracted to the notion of a modern musical that was not trying to be the next *Martin Guerre.* A new musical that was, in many ways, quite traditional would also appeal to the Salisbury audience. Church is not a great fan of musicals in general but liked the way the story was driven by the narrative. The ideas were strong and it worked theatrically.

Wax's timing was perfect. His discussions with Church about presenting *Maddie* at Salisbury took place shortly after Christmas 1995. Church says, 'I always react well to people being enthusiastic, but often they're enthusiastic and unrealistic. Kenny managed to be enthusiastic, realistic and practical.' Church was in a planning cycle with the Playhouse Board at the time, and was able to run the idea past them very quickly. They approved it.

A contract was drawn up, establishing a budget - how much the theatre would put up and how much Wax would have to find - and *Maddie* was finally set to open at the Salisbury Playhouse in September 1996. For a theatre the size of Salisbury Playhouse, with limited funding, *Maddie* was a substantial investment. Church and Wax worked closely together and Wax was able to offer the right balance of funding. The whole project would cost around 100,000 - split equally between them. In the event of a West End transfer, Salisbury negotiated a smaller royalty than usual on a co-production because, as Church puts it, 'Kenny's involvement boosted the quality and scale of the work we do here immeasurably.'

Preparations went on apace. The creative team was joined by Musical Director Martin Lowe, another up-and-coming West End character. Lowe graduated from Hull University in 1989 and had been Assistant MD on the London productions of *Moby Dick, Nine* and *Which Witch?* as well as MD on the 1993 UK tour of *Cats*. He was later to open the 1995 London production of *Cats*, on which he remained musical supervisor.

[Martin Lowe went on to win a Tony, Obie and Drama Desk award for his work on Once *at the Phoenix Theatre. His other work includes* War Horse, Caroline or Change, Mamma Mia *and* Jerry Springer:The Opera. *SMcK]*

Caroline Humphris undertook the orchestrations. Humphris had recently arranged several Sondheim songs for Maria Friedman's Olivier award-winning *By Special Arrangement, Polishing the Sun* for the Noel Gay organisation, Dexter's production of *The Fly* and McKenna's show *Give A Girl A Break* with Guy Kitchenn.

[Caroline Humphris is now one of the UK's leading Musical Directors, Arrangers and Orchestrators with long associations with the National Theatre, the Menier Chocolate Factory, the West End and Broadway. SMcK]

To design the show, Wax chose Niki Turner, who had already designed a number of productions for Salisbury (including *The Crucible, The Rover* and *The Banished Cavaliers*) as well as a host of other regional credits. She was familiar with the Salisbury stage - which is extremely wide and challenging to design for.

The team was in place and the production was booked. Risks remained. Would they get a good cast? Could they attract national critics? Would anybody from the industry travel all the way to Salisbury to see it?

STAR

Now I'm gonna shine...
Just you wait and see..

Wax was always adamant that there were two areas on which he would never compromise. The first was the West End theatre that *Maddie* would eventually transfer to. This could not be too small, for the reasons already discussed, nor could it be too large, or the show would seem swamped by the theatre. However, at this stage a West End transfer was still merely a possibility. First, the team had to get the Salisbury production right.

The second no-compromise area was the casting of the central role. Particularly after having seen Caroline O'Connor's knockout performance at the Lilian Bayliss, Wax was aware that he needed a star performer to play Jan/Maddie. She had to be funny, have a huge voice to tackle songs the size of *Star* and *From Now On*, she needed to move well, and she needed to be an actress of subtlety and versatility to tackle the dual personalities. As the show hinges on the audience's belief that Maddie really did have what it takes to become a movie star, she also needed that special, indefinable quality which makes the audience adore her.

There were surprisingly few performers in their twenties or early thirties who had all the necessary qualities. The UK's big name musical theatre stars - Elaine Paige, Marti Webb, Stephanie Lawrence - had come up through *Evita* and were now too old for the role. Maria Friedman was not interested. There was the added complication that this was a risky proposition - an out of town production of a new show by a new team - and there was no guarantee of a West End transfer.

Caroline O'Connor was starring in *Mack and Mabel* at the Piccadilly Theatre, giving a performance which had attracted wonderful notices and which had been her 'breakthrough' role in terms of public recognition. Caroline had been involved with *Maddie* several times over the years and she had once told McKenna that she thought it would be her breakthrough role. Now, Mabel had done that for her. The team believed that she was about the only person they knew, or knew of, in the business who could do justice to the Jan/Maddie role. Wax approached her.

O'Connor felt that leaving *Mack and Mabel* to do *Maddie* was a risk that she was not prepared to take. Her show was continuing to run, she had made her name in it, she was earning good money and she had the opportunity to build on everything that was going for her. To go out of town for three hundred pounds a week, with no guarantee of a transfer, was something that she did not feel was right for her at this stage in her career.

This was a blow. It became a case of mounting a 'search for a star' - ironically, just as film producer Hugo Dahl does during the course of *Maddie*. Wax faxed all the top agents a list of the four major characters, with the emphasis on Maddie. 'Kenneth Wax is looking for a very funny actress, with a big voice to play American (San Francisco) in her early thirties/late twenties with a big personality and a great sense of comedy.'

Summer Rognlie was an American actress from San Francisco who had just arrived in the UK to see what opportunities there were here for her. She had been playing Grizabella in *Cats* in a tour of Europe.

Rognlie writes:

> I had been living in Hamburg for a year with my husband, Martyn Axe. He had been the musical director of *Cats* while I was on tour over there. Our contracts were finishing and we decided to move back to the States when they were over. Martyn and I travelled to London from Germany in January 1996 to say goodbye to his family and friends. We were moving to my home town of San Francisco to start anew. It was my first visit to London and I loved it. I said to Martyn that if there were anyplace other than California I could live, it would be London. We returned to Germany to finish off our contracts and to prepare ourselves for our return to the States.
>
> Suddenly, the show I was in backed out of its contractual extension and refused to pay us for our last two months of work! I was scheduled to tour with the show until the end of March, when we would be taking all my savings to set us up in California. During this time, Martyn had been offered *Starlight Express* in London, so we decided we had to return to London, where the work was.
>
> We came back to London in May to find a flat. I stayed on with friends while Martyn again returned to Germany, where he was due to complete his contract on June 2nd. Apart from flat-hunting, I wanted to get myself some work. While I was living out of friends' flats, I auditioned for an agent - Jane Wynn Owen at Talent Artists.

On the very day that Wynn-Owen decided to take Rognlie on, Wax's fax regarding *Maddie* arrived on her desk. She still had Rognlie's photograph in front of her. She looked at Rognlie, looked back at the fax and, as she put the actress's CV and photograph in an envelope, she had a strong intuition that this was the future Jan/Maddie.

Rognlie continues:

> Jane called me and gave me the breakdown and I remember saying to her in a Californian squeal, 'Oh my God, this is me!' It sounded perfect - the character was even from San Fracisco! I remember thinking, 'Oh well, if I can't actually be in San Francisco, being in a show that takes place there is the next best thing.' It was my first audition in London, my first agent submission and I was still living out of a suitcase, moving from flat to flat, until our furniture arrived and we could move into our own place. I had only been in London for a week.

The next morning, Wax's assistant, Emma Katz, was opening the mound of photographs and CVs which had arrived from agents. She opened one, looked at the glossy 10x8 photograph and said, 'That's the girl for you.' Kenny looked at it, agreed that she looked fun and thought it would be interesting to see her work.

The first set of auditions, at Sadlers Wells, were scarcely a week later. The team saw a large number of very good people, but nobody who quite had that extra something that they were looking for. Rognlie arrived. Kenny thought that she had a great face, but not the usual West End leading lady face - she had a much more interesting look about her. In his mind he pigeonholed her as a potential Sally.

Rognlie delivered a very funny comic speech and sang *The Music That Makes Me Dance* from *Funny Girl* with gusto. She left the room. On the audition panel that day were Connor, Wax and

Keeling. Connor and Keeling looked at each other, looked back at Wax and said, 'That's the girl for us. She's Maddie.'

Wax's immediate response was 'You've got to be joking! Her? As our leading lady?!' Before the words were out of his mouth, he remembered his determination that he would cast the central role right - even if it was someone with no track record and no reputation in the UK.

Rognlie writes:

> For the first time ever in my life, I felt a perfect affinity with a role. In every other audition I had always tried to fit another type or to be something other than I was. For the first time I thought, 'This *is* me! They *can't* give it to anyone else.' It felt so right - so 'meant to be.' I hadn't heard back from the first audition. I returned to Germany for a few days to help pack the van and move everything to London. The *moment* we arrived at our new flat in London, with all our furniture, I was just unlocking the front door when the telephone rang. It was my agent, telling me I had a recall.

Rognlie's recall was in front of the same panel plus Dexter, McKenna and Toguri. During the week since the first audition, Wax thought more and more about Rognlie and became more and more enthusiastic about seeing her a second time. He trusted Connor and Keeling's judgement and was looking forward to the input of the others. Rognlie sang *A Call From the Vatican* from *Nine* and also reprised *The Music That Makes Me Dance,* which hugely impressed the panel. She read a couple of scenes from the script and nobody could take their eyes off her. She was funny, witty, tender and sexy. McKenna, Toguri and Wax were now sold on the idea, and only Dexter wanted to keep looking - it was, after all, fairly early on in the audition process.

Rognlie was also being offered a role in *Laughter on the 23rd Floor*, starring Gene Wilder, which was heading for a guaranteed West End run after a short national tour. She had been in the country a month and was already in demand. There was a danger that the team might lose her. After calling her back once more to read scenes with potential Nicks, it was decided to make a formal offer.
She accepted. The offer arrived on June 14th 1996 - exactly 70 years to the day that Madeline Marsh was killed - June 14th 1926.

Rognlie recalls:

> The whole thing, coming to London, *Maddie,* all felt so fated. Everything just seemed to fall into place so quickly and smoothly as if it were all meant to be.

The other crucial roles were Nick, Al and Mrs van Arc. For Al, a man in his late seventies, Wax had always been keen to employ a genuinely older actor. Patrick Cargill had been pencilled in since the London showcase but had sadly passed away in the interim. This was felt to be an opportunity to find a good name, perhaps an ageing television star. A large number of people were seen, some famous and some not. It was offered and turned down.
Casting an actor in his seventies carried certain risks - physically, would he be able to handle a demanding singing role for eight performances a week - and could he still bring the necessary energy to the role.

From the outset, Kevin Colson had been interested. Colson was one of the West End's leading older men, famously having taken over from Roger Moore before the first night of *Aspects of Love* and subsequently nominated for a Tony for his performance on Broadway. Colson, though, was only in his fifties - a very robust, handsome man at that. Wax met him, found him extremely charming, and acknowledged that he had been impressed by his performance in *Aspects*, in which he aged during the course of the show.

Colson remembers:

> My agent was getting married and her superior was having a baby so the appointment to meet *Maddie*'s 'family' was passed on through an agency junior. Not for the first time, this resulted in some confusion. Suffice it to say that actor/agent relations are not enhanced by weddings and babies... So, to my date with *Maddie* - a Tuesday at noon in a studio off Holborn - and I was running late (a particular talent of mine)... Perspiring profusely, and on the point of heart and lung failure, I staggered up the last flight of stairs to the designated waiting area (on the dot of noon) to be confronted by a gaggle of 'girlie-twirlies' (theatre-speak for dancers) in various stages of undress, undulating their supple bodies into unbelievably contorted shapes which I am sure served some purpose but to me seemed unnecessarily tortuous. How could this be called a 'warm-up?' Still, it did give me something to look at while I waited... and waited... and waited. One by one the girls were called in to audition and I was ignored. Finally, I accosted the assistant who was calling in the auditionees and asked if my interview was imminent. His list was consulted, and a confused look of consternation crossed his face as he disappeared through the studio doors. Moments later, a slightly perplexed young schoolboy emerged, saying, 'My, *you're* keen.' As this was

obviously Maddie's kid brother playing truant from school, I humoured him by replying enigmatically, 'Why?' I couldn't think of anything else to say. 'Because,' he said, 'we were expecting you tomorrow - but come in anyway.' So I met Maddie's 'family.'

At a long table were seated another kid brother, who turned out to be the composer, Stephen Keeling, several older and wiser uncles (the writers and director) and a choreographer (David Toguri) who smiled benignly and nodded sagely (I thought he might be sleeping but I smiled back anyway!) The young lad who had invited me in turned out to be the producer, Kenny Wax.

Surprisingly, they seemed to know all about me and even more surprisingly, they didn't want to examine my qualifications (so much for preparing an audition piece and warming up the old voice - something which had made me late, sorry, *early*, in the first place). No. *They* auditioned for *me*... telling me the *Maddie* story in some detail and playing me one of the songs that Al Turner sings - Al being my alter-ego should I be accepted into the family. This was encouraging but there seemed to be a problem about my age (which was understandable and a subject I usually avoided). But this time it was not that I was too *old*... I was too *young* by almost twenty years - Al Turner was 75 years old.

Although they had seen me play George Dillingham in *Aspects of Love*, a character who aged to 78, they needed time to think about it. So we bid our farewells and I returned to the real world - already in love with Maddie but so far unrequited.

The day's confusion reminded me of a story Huw

> Weldon told against himself. Arriving punctually at the appointed hour for a black-tie dinner in Eaton Square, Belgravia, he rang the bell and after some delay the door was opened by his hostess wearing a bathrobe and in some disarray. 'Forgive me, my dear,' he said, 'Is it *next* Thursday?' 'No,' she replied gently, 'it was *last* Thursday - and you were here!'
>
> And so I waited... and waited... and waited, but this time there were no 'girlie-twirlies' to distract me. Other (older) potential Al Turners were sought, found and rejected for reasons of unavailability, senility, impending mortality or sheer bloody-mindedness, which often affects us septuagenarians (I say 'us' because after nine weeks of waiting for a response to my interview I felt particularly bloody-minded and *well* old enough to play the role). I duly instructed my agent (back from her honeymoon but now pregnant!) to pass this observation on to the 'family.'

Colson was sent the script and almost immediately declared that he would be delighted to do it. He was to become the anchor of the show. As well as being remarkably talented, Colson proved a marvellous company member and his calm but creative style added greatly to the texture of the piece.

A similar process occurred with the casting of Mrs van Arc. Because she is possessed by Maddie in the second act, it needed an actress who could conceivably have played Maddie twenty or thirty years before. She also had to be credible as the svelte, sophisticated society hostess. Toguri was keen on Angela Richards, who had knocked McKenna for six back in the 1970s when she sang *Surabaya Johnny* on a BBC Omnibus programmed dedicated to the songs of Bertholt Brecht and Kurt Weill and, again, as Eve opposite Lauren Bacall in *Applause,* the musical version of *All About Eve.* More recently, Richards had starred in *Blood Brothers* and, incidentally, wittily performed some of McKenna's material in 1994's *Mercury Workshop Musical Revue.* The team was delighted when she accepted the role.

Finding a Nick proved remarkably difficult. He needed to be in his early 30s, good-looking, charming and able to handle witty dialogue effectively. Many actors playing West End leads were seen. What became very noticeable was that there were plenty of handsome men with sensational voices but very few who could handle text. For a decade or more, the West End had been dominated by sung-through musicals and this had had an effect on performers - they had not *needed* to be able to play dialogue in order to play Marius in *Les Miserables* or Raoul in *Phantom of the Opera.* It was decided to concentrate the search on actors who could sing rather than musical theatre leading men.

Having cast Colson and Richards, two good West End names, and having a sensational newcomer in Rognlie, Wax was determined that Nick should not be 'under-cast' in terms of billing. One actor accepted the role, but his father's ill-health meant he had to return to Australia and so became unavailable for the relevant dates. Some well-known faces were seen, including a couple of Australian soap opera stars, but nobody was right. There was scarcely a fortnight to go before rehearsals began on August 5th 1996.

Mark McGann was a long shot. One of the famous quartet of acting brothers, he was exactly right for the role. McGann had a pleasing light baritone, had played leading roles in musicals before (including John Lennon in *Lennon* at the Astoria and Mickey in *Blood Brothers* at the Phoenix) as well as his many TV and film credits. McGann met Wax and Connor, read the script and - less than a week before rehearsals began - accepted the role.

Wax was thrilled. The addition of McGann to the line-up, both because of his qualities as an actor and his 'name' value, meant that *Maddie* was opening with a company any repertory theatre would be proud to field. The writers, too, felt that the high level of casting - all working for very little money because they liked the piece - was a credit to the quality of the show they had created. Their confidence was further boosted when Lisa Parke at Warner-Chappell agreed to publish the score, giving them an advance against royalties.

A splendid supporting cast of six was put together, with Yvonne Edgell as Sally, Beth Tuckey as Mrs Klein, David Credell as Hugo Dahl, Daniel Coll as O'Hara and Jon Rumney as the comic waiter and Irving, the security guard at Pavilion Pictures.

A young actress was cast as the ghost of Maddie but, after the read-through, was concerned that she had so few lines. She wanted to pull out and Wax generously released her from the contract, feeling this was better for the morale of the show. She was replaced by Hattie Ladbury, who had just graduated from Guildhall School of Music and Drama where she had worked with Martin Connor. She had also assisted Connor at *Maddie* auditions, reading in for potential Nicks. Connor telephoned Ladbury at midnight on the first day of rehearsals and she was in the rehearsal room at ten the next morning. To make this an even more satisfactory first job for Ladbury, she hailed from Salisbury and had made many appearances at the Playhouse with the Salisbury Youth Theatre.

While the casting process was underway, two other key elements of the production were being developed.

When Niki Turner came to design the set for the wide but shallow Salisbury stage - with the caveat that it might need to transfer to a proscenium-arch West End theatre - she studied the script carefully. Her first instinct was to capture the mood and something of the look of old movies - Maddie's 1920s style. This led to the design being principally in black and white, adding splashes of colour in individual pieces of scenery and in the costumes. This filmic quality also extended to finding a sense of fluidity for a large number of scenes and keeping the production moving visually. Turner made preliminary drawings for each scene and, after exploring a number of options, decided that a revolving stage would be preferable to movable trucks. A revolve also provided interesting staging possibilities for Connor and Toguri, using actors walking against the revolve.

There are many different kinds of revolving stage - including a full revolve, an outer or an inner ring only, an independent outer and inner ring, etc. Turner had to decide which kind would best suit her concept and settled on a full revolve, which had to be built and fitted on to the Salisbury stage.

With this in place, everything else, except furniture, was flown. A scene could be set up on the rear of the revolve, behind a backdrop, while the previous scene was playing. This brought the action physically forward, gaining intimacy. Some clever solutions were found in full-stage scenes. In the sound studio at Pavilion Pictures, for example, the balustrade used in the final scene, set on a hotel terrace, was preset in the studio and covered with drapes and props, which were easily removed for the end of the show.

Caroline Humphris was orchestrating Keeling's score for a six piece band - Martin Lowe on piano and keyboards, Juliet McCarthy on cello, Ed Morris on double bass, Scott Povey on flute, clarinet and tenor sax, Paul Stevens on clarinet and soprano sax and Dave Webster on percussion.

After Humphris first heard the music, played on tape by Keeling, she read the script, thought about the Salisbury Playhouse and had a long meeting with Connor in a Soho coffee bar. *Maddie* seemed to her an intimate piece about relationships - and she only had a budget for six musicians. She wanted to make the show sound unique, with a different flavour from the standard small band. She decided early on to use a 'cello. This is not a commonly used instrument. It has a haunting, plaintive sound with a slightly old-fashioned quality which worked well for the older-style numbers.

Humphris' task was made harder because the company was rehearsing in Fulham while she was working on the orchestrations at home in North London. She found herself on the telephone to Martin Lowe two or three times a day, as things changed dramatically. Faxes were exchanged, it seemed, almost hourly. She was working sixteen hours a day and also conducting the West End run of Sondheim's *Passion* in the evenings. This went on for more than four weeks, with Humphris working essentially from scratch - having just Keeling's own piano arrangements to work from. Sometimes communications broke down, exacerbating Humphris' problems. Keeling was also under pressure to write the incidental music, much of which could not be composed until the stage action was set. Batches of new music and scene-change links arrived on Humphris' fax machine.

Her working relationship with Keeling was one of mutual trust. Keeling was amenable to Humphris taking quite a radical approach to his music - which other composers might have baulked at - not in terms of altering melodies but in the 'feel' of the songs. Keeling had not given many orchestration ideas when writing out the score and Humphris found many of the tunes very adaptable - there were choices in the way they could be set and used. Humphris experimented with different styles, different moods and different harmonies - she found it a very creative experience. In *Easy*, Humphris gave the song a much jazzier feel. 'Jazzy' was to prove a keynote description of the tone which Humphris brought to the entire score - it seemed to be the route which most naturally suited the show.

◆ ◆ ◆

Rehearsals began at the Dance Attic in Fulham, a pleasant venue with a handy coffee bar for emergency script discussions. The mood was buoyant on August 5th when the four principals came together for the first time, and the buzz was even stronger when the whole company met for the first time the following Monday.

Colson recalls:

> I was late (!) on the first day and discovered the newly-expanded 'family' greeting one another and desperately trying to remember names. I joined them. It was delightful to see Angela Richards, with whom I had first worked in *Robert and Elizabeth* at the Lyric Theatre in 1965. Others who were strangers soon became friends and a rehearsal of some promise beckoned. After looking at the set and costume designs we read through the script and Stephen Keeling wove in the music and songs he'd completed. It was a work in progressive development and the whole team were always open to consideration of our fanciful variations. An exciting prospect.

Charmian Hoare arrived as Dialect Coach to ensure the consistency of the Californian accent. An interesting challenge faced Richards and Rognlie - how to make their individual performances of Maddie sound and move like the same character.

McGann is a fine and subtle actor but in rehearsal did not always seem comfortable with the genre. He and Rognlie explored the marital relationship in great depth, but this proved very time-consuming and other areas of the show were put under pressure.

Colson comments:

> Following a break for lunch on the first day, our director, Martin Connor, informed us that he would immediately proceed with a rough and ready blocking of the piece, which he had pre-determined for the sake of time. Would we bear with this preliminary sketching of the play till we returned to each scene in more detail? In view of the limited rehearsal time we had available for a brand new musical, I thought this a reasonable request. We had four weeks - *Martin Guerre* had sixteen weeks and then closed during the run for re-staging.
>
> So we agreed - or so I thought. Three weeks later we were still doing initial blocking of the play, and that was just Mark McGann's scenes! Every nuance and blink of an eye was discussed at length (how do you spell *ad nauseam?*) so that some of us didn't get a look in - sometimes not even the director. I just hobbled on, did a turn and hobbled off to bury myself in a good book or go for a long walk. At the time I thought hobbling would be an interesting trait for old Al, though it needed some refinement - still does! We all make mistakes.
>
> I managed to avoid crossing swords with Mark, though I came close when he drew me aside at an early stage of rehearsal and protested that he was having difficulty coming to terms with my interpretation of Al. It was nothing like *he* had imagined the character when preparing for rehearsals and he suggested I consider other options. Fortunately, we

were called to rehearse before he could elaborate on his observations and, strange as it may seem, I never did get round to a more detailed discussion of his version of Al. I wonder... Do you think it could have been the hobbling?

◆ ◆ ◆

Martin Lowe, the Musical Director, had known about *Maddie* for a long time having been friends with Keeling (they both come from Stoke) and having written the opening of Act Two of *The Challenge*. When he first read the script, he responded to the serious issues he felt lay beneath the funny surface. He and Caroline Humphris had known of each other for years without having met. He found working with her and Keeling enormously satisfying, though stressful, and describes it as:

> a steep learning curve. I'd never experienced that level of stress before. As soon as you try to put on a new full-scale musical somewhere other than in the West End, you realise why it doesn't happen often - because of the hours involved and the people you need to do it. Not being in the West End, Caroline and I were taking on the work of an assistant MD, copyists etc as well as our own roles. But if you take on a project like this, you just have to do it.
>
> I think the brief changed during the Salisbury process. What initially attracted me to the show was that it was an intimate chamber piece - it was different to anything anyone else was doing. The fundamental question is, 'How big a show is *Maddie*?' During rehearsals and into the Salisbury run, it seemed that people wanted much more of a big Broadway sound - and Caroline's original orchestrations were not really in that genre.
>
> In some respects this show is a MDs dream because it covers seventy years of singing styles. Summer and I spent hours listening to singers from different periods to get the changes of style right. Maddie's singing patterns start with the 1920s style (which is all she knows when she first reappears) of *I'll Find Time For You*. As she spends longer in the modern world,

> the sounds of that world start to influence her. We worked hard and long on charting that development, so that the first big 'Broadway belt' was right at the end of *Star*. We worked together to create a vocal journey.
>
> It all started to go slightly wrong for me during the few days up to the opening performances, when it seemed as if the goalposts were moved. Instead of being a chamber piece, the thrust moved firmly towards the Broadway sound. While I could academically have defended everything we were doing, I could also understand why the rest of the team wanted to go in the direction we now seemed to be heading.

Towards the end of the first week of rehearsals, a discussion arose about including an ensemble comedy number at the gates of Pavilion Pictures. This had been mooted many times over the years but it was always felt that the dialogue scene was very funny and it would not be possible to know whether a song would improve matters until it was on the floor. Having blocked the scene, Connor felt that it would give Act Two a jolt of energy. McKenna and Keeling set to, sending drafts to Connor, Wax and Dexter (who was deep in rehearsals for his production of Harman and Herrmann's *Romance, Romance*) at the Bridewell Theatre. Several versions were written and the team finally settled on one which went, in part:

MADDIE: *I've got more talent in my little finger*
Than this dumb kid could show in forty years.
NICK/AL *I'm sorry, she's a washed-up, ageing swinger.*
MADDIE *I'm a humdinger!*
IRVING/AL *It'll all end in tears.*

JAN	*Oh Mama, please Mama,*
	Don't spoil my big chance!
IRVING	*Your mother?...*

As a result of adding an ensemble in Act Two, and given the singing talents of the assembled company, Connor felt strongly that another ensemble number should be added in Act One to balance the Gate Song. Keeling came up with the idea of reinstating *Blame It On Mama,* which had not been heard since the Oxford masterclasses. McKenna adjusted the lyric and the accompanying scene, giving Sally a more central role, as this would replace her duet with Jan, *Never Gonna Speak To Him Again.*

The opening number, *How In The World* also proved problematic. In it, Nick and Jan were so confrontational that their marriage seemed not just slightly stale and edgy, but almost at the point of divorce (or murder!). The spin-off effect was to alienate the audience's sympathy from Jan - the song, plus some of her dialogue, made her seem whiny and hard. The lyric was rewritten and the melody softened. Jan's opening verse:

I don't like confrontation,
I just want to see fair play.
It's a tough situation
And getting worse every day.
'Cos I don't feel he values me.
How in the world am I gonna make him see?

became:

I thought, just for a minute,
He might leap to my defence,
Fight my corner, help win it -
I should have had a little more sense.
'Cos I don't feel he values me.
How in the world am I gonna make him see?

The team would continue to play with these elements right up to the first weekend of the run.

After two weeks full company rehearsals in London, the company moved to Salisbury and completed rehearsals in Moose Hall - with the huge-antlered, stuffed head of a dead moose staring balefully down on the proceedings.

The first act was running at nearly an hour and a half - at least fifteen minutes too long. Some nips and tucks were taken and a major cut proposed in the morning after scene which, fortunately, Rognlie and McGann adamantly opposed. It was to become one of the funniest scenes in the Salisbury production.

By the time the first dress rehearsal approached, it was clear that Sondheim had been right about *Blame It On Mama* all along - it felt like a song from a different show. The focus of the show now rather abruptly cut away from Nick and Jan's situation (with which the audience were very involved) to provide a lively irrelevance. This broke the dramatic tension and made it harder to Rognlie to recapture the audience for her Act One barnstormer, *Star. Blame It On Mama* had to go. This was no reflection on the dedication and aplomb of the company who were singing it for all they were worth.

There was insufficient time to write, rehearse and orchestrate a new number for opening night and there was discussion of whether the entire scene should be cut. However, having given the company an ensemble number in a show which was otherwise for only four voices, it was felt that morale could be severely affected by such a move. It was also impossible, given the design, to move straight from the apartment to the downtown San Francisco set. McKenna and Keeling set to work on a replacement therapy song ready to be rehearsed on the Monday of the second week of the run. This was much gentler and more hippy-dippy:

> *If you amend your attitude*
> *And show a little gratitude*
> *You'll find you have the strength to start anew.*
> *Sure, you want to make him suffer.*
> *Pain is tough but, Jan, you're tougher.*
> *This is what to do.*
> *Concentrate on you.*

◆ ◆ ◆

Kevin Colson recalls:

> By the time we were nearing first performances of *Maddie*, I had fallen in love again. Not that knee-jerking, palpitating rush of blood that restricts your breathing and makes the mind hallucinate. Just a warm and pleasurable sensation of performing with, and being in the presence of, a remarkable and incandescent talent that was a joy to behold. Call it Sum-

> mer love, but I was smitten. Our leading lady was coming into her own and I couldn't wait for the critics and the public to confirm my opinion. Awesome, as my sons would say.

Technical and dress rehearsals are tense on every show - everyone realises that they need twenty four hours longer to achieve their goals. The *Maddie* technical was no exception and the first dress rehearsal on Wednesday September 4th was a disaster. Scene changes appeared to be taking decades rather than moments, the cast were exhausted and trying to compensate by over-projecting songs and characters, the music drowned the singers and the throat-mikes could not, it seemed, be satisfactorily balanced against the band. Costume changes were slow and there was a problem with the fold-back - the onstage speakers through which the performers hear the orchestra.

Opening night, which was technically *Maddie*'s one and only preview, was remarkably respectable under the circumstances. The audience responded warmly. Jonathan Church and the Playhouse team seemed pleased. The only stand-up row of the entire production took place in the Circle Bar when the entire creative team left the first night party to discuss putting in the new therapy song. Everyone was exhausted and tense and after opening night nerves. Tempers flared. It was quite a spectacle!

◆ ◆ ◆

Jonathan Church, Artistic Director of the Salisbury Playhouse, recalls:

> People responded well to the bold decision to open our season with *Maddie.* It was an unusual step and also a risk - this was our first full year of programming, running from September through to July. My honeymoon year as Artistic Director was over and it was healthy to have some outside input at this point. We were trying to put on a new show with the theatre being rebuilt (thanks to a lottery grant) around us. The foyer was in chaos, the box office in a portakabin and a foyer extension in a tent. There was a buzz in the building which was projecting itself out into the local media by the time *Maddie* opened.
>
> They genuinely enjoyed *Maddie* and it genuinely

worked as an evening. The audience entered into the spirit of a new show that was still being tried out. Indeed, some people came back a second or third time to see what changes had been made. This is one of the benefits of an audience that you have a long-standing relationship with.

We at Salisbury also felt we had an artistic investment in the piece. Kenny and Martin had chosen Niki Turner from a list that the three of us had compiled. It was good to work with her again - it added to the feel of *Maddie* being a Salisbury show. We also had full production management responsibility - we built the set, made the costumes and were responsible for all the stage management.

There were surprisingly few problems - sometimes the response time to changes and suggestions seemed slow, but there were so many collaborators that every major alteration had to be approved by.

◆ ◆ ◆

The local press were expected on the second night and the local critics were scheduled to attend during the first week. In the meantime, the new song was rehearsed and inserted, and some changes were made to the opening of the show.

As it seemed to take a long time for the story to really begin, *How In The World* was cut completely. A more controversial cut was the choreographed Prologue which showed Maddie and the Blue Belles on the stage of the Alcazar theatre in 1926. This had been planned to say to the audience, 'This is musical comedy,' but the design placed it too far upstage and made it too small. There was sound artistic thinking for this - it was as if the audience were seeing the moment through the wrong end of a telescope, looking back through fifty years. The Prologue, though, also added two or three more minutes to an already over-long first half.

The opening dialogue between Sally, Nick and Jan was not funny enough - and the new therapy scene was only a marginal improvement on *Blame It On Mama.* Lengthy scene changes broke the flow of the second act and did not help the performers to build up the necessary head of steam to make the farce work.

However, all reservations aside, it was clear that *Maddie* was capturing the audience's imagination. Most of it worked just as the writers had imagined. Applause was long and warm. It took the show about a week to settle in, after which Rognlie regularly raised the roof with *Star* and Richards came into her own to give a splendid comic performance. The great surprise of the show was Kevin Colson's Al. His performance was the bedrock of the show, a performance of marvellous subtlety, wit, warmth and immense sexuality. Lines which McKenna and Dexter had written almost casually, suddenly acquired layers of depth and poignancy. His final moments were heart-rending - and snuffles could be heard coming from around the auditorium.

Morale rose higher and higher among the exhausted company as they gradually realised that there were in a hit show. A hit show, moreover, that had a real chance of a London run. It was also clear, as the team had always believed, that Rognlie was proving a very bright star indeed.

◆ ◆ ◆

Martin Lowe recalls:

> Very early on, the band caught on to the fact that this show had a very funny script and a great story. Indeed, there were a few scenes where, every night, they would put down their books and watch, still laughing at the jokes after two or three weeks. That doesn't happen very often.

The local reviews were uniformly excellent:

> "Its starry cast... meets expectations, it has a touch of Sondheim in its pedigree, and it is bursting with great songs in a structured, if far-fetched, storyline. Star of the show is Summer Rognlie who lights it up with her personality and stunning voice... The book, lyrics and music trio of Shaun McKenna, Steven Dexter and Stephen Keeling creates a musical that is a romance, a ghost story, deliciously witty, a romping comedy and a focus on the serious side of human nature." *Salisbury Journal*

> "The capacity first night crowd for *Maddie* certainly enjoyed it very much. It's easy to see why - it's very funny, it is touching, it has an excellent witty script, it is well-acted and sung, the direction is crisp and

pacy, the sets are clever, it has some first-rate performances and the music is the hummable side of Stephen Sondheim... Whether *Maddie* will make it to the West End - or, even more crucially, make it IN the West End - is anybody's guess. But it deserves to." *Blackmore Vale Magazine*

"This is a musical with a big warm heart, a great storyline, memorable tunes... and it's very funny... The night belongs to Summer Rognlie. She is, quite simply, a star as she slips effortlessly from the provoked Jan Cheyney to the provoking Maddie Marsh, with a singing voice that can coo like Monroe and soar like Streisand." *Bournemouth Evening Echo*

"The storyline alone and the superb acting could earn this show a place in stage history and make a star of the brilliant Rognlie..." *New Forest Post*

"Hearing and seeing a big West End musical like *Maddie* in Salisbury Playhouse is an overpowering experience. American star Summer Rognlie is like six Barbra Streisands and an Ethel Merman rolled into one. Her Act I curtain number, *Star*, is done with all the force and absolute mastery of the block-buster musical tradition. Alone worth the price of admission... Kevin Colson as Maddie's lover of long ago provides the emotional heart of the story with his tremendously sensitive acting and singing... Angela Richards as Cordelia van Arc is an only slightly less explosive belter than Miss Rognlie... It will be a long time before we will see the like of it at Salisbury Playhouse again." *Avon Advertiser*

There were around fifteen further local reviews, all essentially saying the same thing.

Business was reasonably good, certainly matching the target set by the Playhouse. The first week was slow, as most of the reviews did not appear for almost a week after the opening, but picked up tremendously thereafter. The Playhouse had not produced a musical for seven years, and the genre had never been the Salisbury audience's first choice.

Jonathan Church comments:

> We had a reasonable but not spectacular advance - an unknown show led to caution. Word of mouth soon kicked in and we went on to enjoy one of the liveliest booking periods we'd ever had for a show that was currently playing.

It was clear to the team that 75% of the show worked very well, 10% could bear technical improvement and 15% needed to be re-written before a West End transfer.

The question of whether *Maddie* could attract the national critics was important. Until the notices were in, the team had no endorsement of how good the show was. They believed in it with all their hearts but to grab the attention of potential co-producers and investments, the reaction of the powerful national newspapers was all-important. Cameron Duncan, Wax's press agent, worked enormously hard and managed to attract the leading critics from *The Times, The Sunday Times* and *The Daily Telegraph.*

First to appear was John Peter's notice in the *Sunday Times*:

> "This enjoyable and hugely promising musical... Shaun McKenna and Steven Dexter's book needs a little tightening but it handles the complicated material with an athletic aplomb. Stephen Keeling's music is crisp and beguiling: he is niftily sophisticated

> when he is composing spoofs of various periods... The actor/singers never put a foot wrong."

This was a good start. *The Stage* came next.

> "People who like musicals will love this show - people who don't like musicals will love it, too. It's a simple as that... Its faults are few and nothing that a nip and a tuck couldn't solve... Star of the show is American actress Summer Rognlie, who lights up this unusual and appealing musical with her stunning voice and charisma... The mayhem also sparks delicious humour, romping comedy, gritty character development and good old spooking. Like all the best musicals, *Maddie* boasts great songs woven into a workable storyline."

Now Wax needed one more great review to clinch interest from the key producers and get them down to see the Salisbury production. The third national review was in *The Times*. It was polite but unenthusiastic, the headline reading, 'A slightly vacant possession.'

> "The resurrection of Maddie is used as an opportunity to create irritated confusions, although now and then a deeper and infinitely more interesting plot breaks through. The 80-year old pianist (Kevin Colson) dances again with the woman he loved, who has stayed stuck at 20... In these peripheral moments it is as if a kraken has swum up from the ocean bed, found the air unfavourable and sunk back. The show arrives at the Playhouse with good credentials, notably the growing reputation of Stephen Keeling, its composer, though I do hanker for tunes to hum. Fashions change, but this is a book musical of the old kind - ie, not a Lloyd Webberian *gesamkuntswerk*, where the instruments never stop. the orchestration

> in *Maddie* provides an emotional charge to memories of what might have been, the urge to make up for lost time, but the absence of instant melody means that the situations and characters do not become permeated and defined by music. Some of the scenes Shaun McKenna and Steven Dexter have written fail to work. The group therapy meeting is not only silly but without function... Summer Rognlie gives a thrilling performance, forthright and feisty, in the Maddie sections of her role."

This review took the proceedings seriously but was not good enough - certainly not what Wax needed. He was beginning to worry whether the industry's powerful figures would travel down the M3. *Maddie* was running for three and a half weeks and the *Times* review did not appear until well into the second week.

The *Telegraph* critic was Charles Spencer. When Connor and McKenna took their seats on press night, they realised that they were sitting behind him and hastily moved to vacant seats on the other side of the theatre. Spencer was sitting in H21. Wax, by coincidence, was watching the show with his uncle and had been allocated H19 and H20. Wax had never met Spencer and had no idea who he was. Spencer scribbled away furiously throughout the performance and laughed frequently. Wax's uncle, in H20, kept nudging his nephew, smiling and giving him the thumbs up. It is not the done thing for producers to speak to critics while they are working, but it was clear from Spencer's comments to Jonathan Church at the end of the evening that he had enjoyed himself. It only remained for his review to appear.

Everyone bought the *Telegraph* every day. Spencer had seen the show in the first week. The second week came and went, then the third. Still, nothing in the *Telegraph*. Eventually, in the final week, Wax was pulling his hair out. He felt they needed one great review in the national press to put *Maddie* on the map. He drove to Kings Cross every night at midnight, to pick up the first edition of the following day's papers.

Wax says:

> Finally, one night I opened the paper and read a review that couldn't have been better if I had written it myself. It was that good. The headline was 'The show we've all been waiting for.' It was ironic, because this was the review that the team had all been waiting for.

Spencer's review was an endorsement from one of the country's most important critics. It brought a lot of people - both the general public and industry insiders - in to see the show. There was a rush for tickets for the final few performances.

Spencer's review read, in part:

> "I don't want to start a frenzy of hype and inflated expectations, but this show could be just what we've been waiting for: a new British musical by previously unknown hands which is blessed with wit, charm and a terrific star performance... *Maddie* strikes me as being about ten times more enjoyable than *Martin Guerre* and easily stands comparison with the Wodehouse/Ayckbourn collaboration *By Jeeves*. The show's creators have realised that audiences are weary of overblown megamusicals: they want humour, romance, and an escape from po-faced portentousness - a return, in fact, to the traditional values of the musical's golden age... Summer Rognlie gives a knockout performance as Jan/Maddie, a single body alternately occupied by two contrasting personalities... The situation is largely played for laughs, but there's poignancy here, too. The scene

in which Maddie meets her former lover, now an old man who has always cherished her memory, is genuinely touching. And there is a real sexual frisson in the fact that Nick finds himself fancying the ghostly interloper more than his wife. This exploration of the illicit workings of desire adds substance to the froth... Stephen Keeling's tuneful score ranges from full-blown showbiz anthems to gentle love songs, and the book, by Shaun McKenna and Steven Dexter, is generously packed with gags and knockabout... Rognlie is a real find as Jan/Maddie. There's never a flicker of doubt about which character she's playing and her leather-lunged voice and ability to combine the sassy with the vulnerable puts me in mind of Liza Minnelli... There are cherishable performances from Kevin Colson... and Angela Richards... There are a few rough edges that need polishing but for the most part Martin Connor directs with the confidence of a man who reckons he's on to a winner - and who can blame him? If the show transfers, as I hope it will, the West End might just go mad about *Maddie*."

The show we've been waiting for

THEATRE
Maddie
Salisbury Playhouse

I DON'T want to start a frenzy of hype and inflated expectations, but this show could be just what we've been waiting for: a new British musical by previously unknown hands which is blessed with wit, charm and a terrific star performance.

So many new musicals have bitten the dust in recent years that one is chary of over-excitement. I can only report that *Maddie* strikes me as being about 10 times more enjoyable than *Martin Guerre* and easily stands comparison with the Wodehouse/Ayckbourn collaboration *By Jeeves*.

The show's creators have realised that audiences are weary of overblown mega-musicals. They want humour, romance and an escape from po-faced portentousness — a return, in fact, to the traditional values of the musical's golden age.

Maddie is blessed with a smashing script, based on a novel by Jack Finney about ghostly possession. But while the novel belonged to the Hollywood Gothic school, the tone here is lighter, reminiscent indeed of Coward's *Blithe Spirit*.

We are in San Francisco in 1981, and the marriage between Nick Cheyney, a museum curator, and his wife, Jan, is drifting in the seven-year doldrums. Redecorating their apartment, they discover a message, written in 1926 by a young Hollywood flapper on the eve of her big movie break. Unfortunately she was killed on her way to the crucial screen test. Now, however, the dead starlet believes she can try again, by possessing the body of Nick's wife.

It's an ingenious and disconcerting conceit. The American actress Summer Rognlie gives a knockout performance as Jan/Maddie, a single body alternately occupied by two contrasting personalities. Jan is repressed and shy, Maddie a feisty exhibitionist.

The situation is largely played for laughs, but there's poignancy here, too. The scene in which Maddie meets her former lover, now an old man who has always cherished her memory, is genuinely touching. And there is a real sexual frisson in the fact that Nick finds himself fancying the ghostly interloper more than his wife. This exploration of the illicit workings of desire adds substance to the froth.

The show was developed at workshops during Stephen Sondheim's Oxford professorship, but owes almost nothing to his sophisticated influence. Stephen Keeling's tuneful score ranges from full-blown showbiz anthems to gentle love songs, and the book, by Shaun McKenna and Steven Dexter, is generously packed with gags and knockabout. My major criticism is of McKenna's sometimes banal and verbose lyrics, which would benefit from an injection of Sondheim's wry dry wit.

Rognlie is a real find as Jan/Maddie. There's never a flicker of doubt about which character she is playing and her leather-lunged voice and ability to combine the sassy with the vulnerable put me in mind of Liza Minnelli. Mark McGann as Nick occasionally seems overshadowed by the sheer force of her personality, but there are cherishable performances from Kevin Colson as Maddie's old admirer and Angela Richards as a rich bitch of a society hostess.

There are a few rough edges that need polishing, but for the most part Martin Connor directs with the confidence of a man who reckons he's on to a winner — and who can blame him? If the show transfers, as I hope it will, the West End might just go mad about *Maddie*.

Tickets: 01722 320333

CHARLES SPENCER

Wax's prayers were answered. His lobbying of producers, aided and abetted by everyone involved in the show, drew independent producers as well as representatives of Cameron Mackintosh, the Really Useful group and Apollo leisure to Salisbury in the final week of the run.

Rognlie recalls:

> My agent went to extreme lengths to get people from London to come and see it. The only way that people from Cameron Mackintosh and Really Useful could come was if they got a lift back to London after the show - the trains didn't run late enough. They took the train down and Jane drove down to Salisbury in the evening simply to pick them up after the show and take them back to London - driving five hours just to do the shuttle. That's devotion to a client!

Jonathan Church comments:

> The *Telegraph* review not only changed the tone of the response nationally, it affected the local audience more than you would imagine. *The Telegraph* is undoubtedly the broadsheet most commonly read by our audience - and Spencer had come to a number of projects at the Playhouse in the preceding months. It is always good when you can attract someone of that status. Many people came to see *Maddie* who had never set foot inside the Playhouse before - we played to one of the broadest cross-sections of
>
> the community ever. Because the project attracted industry attention, some nights in the final week the foyer looked like a *Who's Who?* of British theatre - and our audience got a buzz from that.

During the final week, a nasty bug went through the cast.

Rognlie continues:

> By closing night everybody was ill. Angela Richards was suffering from flu and losing her voice. She was

sucking down hot lemon and Sudafed. Mark McGann had a horrible lung infection and was on antibiotics. He was coughing up blood - not a good thing as we had a lot of heavy duty kissing during the show.

I awoke the Saturday morning of our closing night at 3.30am in excruciating pain. I had the worst earache I had ever had since being a child. Any movement, even a yawn, was unbearable. I felt helpless. I called my Mom in California is tears. I had a cold, which I had been suppressing with decongestants and Sudafed to get through the last week. The whole sickness, unable to release itself, finally accumulated in my ears. I went to the local A&E at 8am explaining that it was closing night and I had to perform two shows that day, hoping the doctor could give me something to get me through it. He looked at my ears in astonishment and told me it was one of the worst ear infections he had ever seen. He put me on major antibiotics with a triple dose to start that morning. I was also to continue taking Sudafed.

The pain had subsided a little by the matinée. As the music started for my first number, *I'll Find Time For You*, I found I could only hear the undertones of the piano. To me it sounds completely flat. I'm totally panicked! I can't hear my notes, or judge the key, or anything. I sang the whole show from body memory - I had no idea if I was on pitch or not!

By the evening performance, I could hear the tones fairly normally. Everything seemed fine until the opening number of the second act, *One More Day*. I couldn't get a sound out! No singing would come. It seemed as though, my voice having relaxed and warmed down during the intermission, my voice had

> left me. I'm playing to a packed house, with important guests, possibly the last time I would ever play the role... I'm dying a million deaths inside. The panic rose inside me as I continued to speak-sing the song. In my mind, I'm thinking we're going to have to stop the show. I still have three big songs to do. I remember looking into the orchestra pit, at Martin Lowe, right before the beginning of the next big number. There seemed to be this momentary pause when we just connected with each other. He looked at me as if to say, 'I'm here. We're going to do this together.' He was talking to the sound department through his headset. They were pumping me up and Martin brought the orchestra way down... He was right on it and I love him for it. Miraculously, somehow my voice came back for the last numbers. After the show, while chatting to everyone at the reception in the foyer, my voice had gone completely. My body, with all the antibiotics and decongestants, had finally given up on me.

The Salisbury run had gone as well as the creative team could have hoped. The burning question was now, 'Does *Maddie* have a future? Will it transfer?'

DON'T LOOK BACK

If I don't look back
I won't see him lie,
If I don't look back
He won't see me cry...

Investing in theatre is notoriously risky. It is generally held that out of five shows, two will incur total losses, two will break even and one will be very successful. Few producers can afford to finance their productions entirely, so they seek angels. The term 'angel' is defined in the Collins Concise Dictionary as 'a spiritual being believed to be an attendant or messenger of God' and as 'an investor in theatrical productions.' A producer would explain these definitions to mean one and the same.

Investing in theatre is more like speculating with stocks and shares than gambling on the horses. The golden rule spelled out in all prospectuses is that you have to be prepared to forfeit your capital and you should not invest what you cannot afford to lose. But with high risk comes the potential for high gain.

Jack Tinker, the late theatre critic for the *Daily Mail*, noted that *Cats* has repaid its investors over 25 times. Put another way, a 750 stake in 1981 had yielded a return of over 20,000 by 1996. Yet in 1981, just before it opened, *Cats*' producer - a young Cameron Mackintosh - simply could not find the investors to back Andrew Lloyd Webber's dance show based on T.S. Eliot's poems. Somehow they scraped together the necessary 600,000 - the rest is history.

The explanation of how it works for the investor is quite simple. An amount of money, called the capitalisation is needed to pay all the salaries and bills to take the show up to West End opening night. Once the show is running it incurs weekly running costs like any business. Providing that these running costs (and the creative team royalties) are covered by the weekly box office revenue, the excess goes straight back to repaying the investors. From the point at which the capital is recouped, the investors will earn their pro-rata share of between 60 - 70% of all the profit from that production of the show.

[In the intervening years, theatre funding has become a great deal more complex. Once upon a time, the creative team took their royalties from the gross box office takings. This means, for instance, a 2% lyrics royalty on a show grossing £100,000 a week would bering the lyricist £2000 a week. In the 1990s the 'royalty pool' system, originating on Broadway where costs are higher, began to creep into the West End agreements too and is now pretty much universal. In the royalty pool system the lyricist's 2% is translated into two points in a pool for all the creatives, a pool normally totalling around 20 points. Rather than receiving royalties on gross income, the pool receives a proportion (usually 25%) of the net profits. So, a show grossing £100,000 a week but costing £60,000 a week to run, provides the creatives with £10,000 and the investors with £30,000. The 2% lyric royalty drops from £2000 a week to £1000. Still a good haul, you might think, but remember that several years unpaid work have gone into making the show and any money the lyricist has received will almost always be largely an "advance" against royalties, clawed back before royalties are paid out. To make this deal more palatable to creatives, producers offer a "minimum guarateee" of, say, £350 a week per royalty point. In this case our lyricist gets a guaranteed £700 a week and the remainder of any royalties once the advances have been paid back. However, the words "minimum" and "guarantee" don't mean what they mean in the rest of the world. The moment the show is not making money, it is expected that the creatives will

waive their royalties altogether, "for the good of the project." If you refuse, pressure is usually brought to bear. "You'll never work in this business again," is not a comedy threat from an old movie. The theatre is a small world. Get a reputation for being difficult and people stop employing you. SMcK]

In addition to the Salisbury Playhouse's financial contribution to *Maddie*, Wax had put in around fifty thousand pounds. That was pretty much all the money he had so far raised, and it had not been easy. If the show had a chance of transferring, he needed to raise something in the region of a further four hundred thousand pounds.

Wax had printed an article in the Salisbury programme, entitled 'Where Angels Dare To Tread'. A considerable number of people expressed an interest in investing. Prospectuses were sent to them. Wax also approached the lighting, sound and other supply companies who were involved in the show. White Light Lighting, Orbital Acoustic Sound and London Musicians, the orchestral managers, all came up with some money on the basis that there are few new shows, and few young producers - they felt if they could afford to, they should give Wax a chance. He was very grateful for their support. He also re-approached previous investors, who often gave him other potential contacts. Even one of the actors in the Salisbury production invested. Money started to come in.

Having twenty five great reviews made a difference to Wax's position when it came to raising money, but he was still underfunded by a substantial amount. One day, he received a telephone call from Adrian Leggatt at Apollo Leisure, who had seen - and liked - the show. Leggatt said that Apollo Leisure would like to co-produce *Maddie* in London, putting up around half the money. Wax was delighted. Lawyers drew up the contract. Leggatt and Wax approached Sir Stephen Waley-Cohen, who owned the Vaudeville Theatre. Waley-Cohen had also seen the show and was keen to have it at his theatre. In an upstairs room at the Vaudeville, he, Wax, Leggatt and Paul Greig, managing director of Apollo Leisure, shook hands on a deal for a March 1997 opening. Wax almost floated down the Strand and phoned the creative team saying that he had a handshake agreement. It was 95% certain that the show would go ahead.

Whilst floating down the Strand, Wax bumped into actor Graham Bickley at a nearby bank cash dispenser.

Bickley recalls:

> I met Kenny at a cash machine on the Strand. He was buzzing with excitement having just secured the cash to finally greenlight a west end production of *Maddie.*
>
> I was at that time playing Joe Gillis at the Adelphi Theatre. We had been given our notice and *Sunset Boulevard* was due to close in a few weeks. I had just been offered the role of 'Beast' in a new production of Disney's *Beauty and The Beast* at The Dominion Theatre. We congratulated each other on our good fortune and Kenny mentioned that had I not been cast, I would have been on his list for the role of Nick. I thanked him for the thought and we wished each other well.
>
> Rehearsals for 'Beast' would overlap with the final fortnight of Sunset, the show was getting huge publicity as the next 'big musical' so I felt very fortunate. But something wasn't right.
>
> My then agent Penny Wesson, had begun negotiations for the contract, and as one would expect, Disney had created a strict format for all productions - principal fees were fixed and they would not be moved. *Sunset Boulevard* had been a joy to play in. A fabulous role, I was rarely off stage. The fee was decent but the biggest

perk was a driver who picked me up and delivered me home each day. Never happened before or since. No wonder the production was losing money!

Disney were having none of that nonsense so the idea of getting myself to and from the theatre reluctantly began to sink in. Welcome back to the real world.

One afternoon, at about that time, I was browsing in Dress Circle, the much lauded Showbiz shop, when an agent approached me, and congratulated me on being cast as Beast. He had a client who was also in the company, and he offered to send me a pirate video of the Vienna production of *Beauty and The Beast.* A few days later, it arrived and I sat at home watching it. My heart sank.

To this day, I am not sure what I expected, but what I saw was an elongated show similar to several I had seen in the Disney Parks. It was slick, clever and polished, but for the first time, I could see clearly what I was signing up for, for a whole year, and my heart just wasn't in it. I specifically remember the end of the first act, where the Beast sings the anthemic *If I Can't Love Her*, with a glorious elongated final note. But the curtain was already in, and Disney trinkets being sold before the Beast had even finished his song!

That same day, Penny Wesson telephoned to say that negotiations were difficult, but they had agreed to decorate the dressing room and provide a TV. My heart sank further. It wasn't about the size of TV or a new coat of paint. I didn't want the role and I had to own up. Eventually, I told Penny, and she suggested I take the weekend to think it over. On the Monday morning, I officially turned the role down.

Unsurprisingly, things started to happen at speed. The casting office simply couldn't accept my decision. No one turns Disney down. Transatlantic telephones calls were made and eventually Guy Kitchenn, whose company Cole Kitchenn were production managing the show in the UK, spoke with me to confirm that the decision was entirely mine, memorably offering me a further £1000 a week as a final incentive to rethink. I thanked him, promising him I wasn't calling anyone's bluff and confirmed my decision.

As news got out, the online theatre forums lit up. According to them I had turned it down due to various reasons, including not accepting £15,000 a week (oh so not correct), my request for a dressing room jacuzzi being turned down (nope) and other more laughable and spurious theories.

I received a call from Cameron Mackintosh's No 2 Nick Allott, congratulating me on my brave and honest decision, which helped me to deal with the fallout. Although I've never worked for them since!

Alasdair Harvey, the actor who replaced me, played the Beast very successfully, and the show won an Olivier Award in 1998. (With a twist of irony, Alasdair co-produced a production of *Kiss Me Kate* a couple of years later, for which I auditioned. I didn't get it!).

To this day, I have no regrets about my decision not to play Beast. The ultimate test was taking my two young nephews to see the show. We all thoroughly enjoyed it, but crucially, there were no pangs. And that bloody curtain still came down early at the end of act one!

◆ ◆ ◆

The creative team set about solving the problems with the show that had emerged at Salisbury. In a series of meetings at Connor's home in Greenwich, the book was tightened, the 'laughs' were analysed, new jokes added and new songs explored.

This was the final stage of re-writing. It was strongly felt that both the opening and close of Act One needed attention. The only major conceptual change, in order to beef up the re-instated Prologue, was to lose all reference to Maddie's dancing partners - Trixie, Lilian and Bea. Instead, Maddie and Al had been a double-act, he playing the piano and dancing a little, while she danced and sang. (This meant minor lyric changes to *Time of My Life*).

The Prologue now begins in 1926, as we see Maddie and Al performing their routine at the Alcazar Theatre. After the curtain comes down, the pair kiss before Maddie exits, leaving Al on a bare stage, holding her straw hat. Lights focus down to a solo spot on Young Al. Another tight spot upstage reveals on the older Al, looking at a similar, battered hat. The stage revolves, bringing old Al downstage, lost in his memories of Maddie. The apartment wall flies in and a knock on the door jolts Al back to the present day - in 1981. Nick and Jan Cheyney are just moving in to the apartment. A choreographic sequence is added as their furniture is put into place. Then Jan discovers the message on the wall.

This was felt to say 'musical comedy' to the audience, and also to give the first fifteen minutes (which had always been slow at Salisbury) much more movement, life and interest.

The team decided that the ensemble *Therapy Song* had to go. At this point in the show, the audience were very involved in the Nick/Jan/Maddie triangle and wanted to follow it through. They had also seen little of Jan since her possession and wanted to know how she felt. Wax felt that the show needed a big emotional duet for Nick and Jan - as a result, *Don't Look Back* was written.

The morning after scene, just before *Don't Look Back*, had been very funny, ending with Al hitting Nick with his walking stick. It was decided that the comedy should continue for a little longer, to counteract the pathos of *Time of My Life* and to prepare the audience for the emotional intensity of *Don't Look Back* and the pizazz of *Star*. Dexter came up with the notion of bringing Mrs Klein to the Cheyney's apartment, to sack Nick. In previous drafts, this had always happened offstage. Beth Tuckey had turned her few lines as Mrs Klein in the Salisbury production into something rather special, and Dexter felt it was a splendid opportunity to give her a scene to complete Mrs Klein's journey. He and McKenna worked on a scene which incorporated some existing funny dialogue and created a series of comic misunderstandings which gave the scene drive and impetus.

After the emotional intensity of *Don't Look Back*, a musicalised and choreographic chase scene was devised, during which Nick follows Jan onto the streets of San Francisco. The *Don't Look Back* theme, one of Keeling's soaring romantic melodies, continues as underscoring.

One problem during *Star* in Salisbury was that Nick was left on stage with nothing very much to do, while Rognlie knocked the audience's socks off. In the new draft, the action follows Maddie inside the cinema, and the Act One curtain is hers alone.

Act Two needed less drastic attention, primarily concentrating on sharpening and adding jokes. Again, Nick was stopped from looking (and feeling) like a spare part by leaving Maddie alone on stage during *From Now On*.

The magic and ghostly effects had been fairly rudimentary at Salisbury - the ghost of Maddie being played by Hattie Ladbury on stilts in a tight spotlight, and re-appearing through a gauze above the apartment set during *From Now On.* Wax decided that, as the show was to be billed as 'a magical new musical' these effects needed greater impact. He recruited the celebrated magician Ali Bongo to supervise the magic effects - and how they were to be achieved remained a close secret.

Niki Turner also had a larger budget to work with on the design. Because of the structural changes to the script, new solutions to design problems had to be found and the apartment itself, where so much of the action takes place, was redesigned to have a warmer and more homely atmosphere.

There were meetings of the creative and technical team at the Vaudeville in the last months of 1996 and excitement was mounting in preparation for the March opening.

◆ ◆ ◆

Rachel Freck, a producer on BBC Radio 2, was planning a series of six half hour programmes on new musicals, each programme concentrating on a single show. The programmes were to be hosted, and the interviews conducted, by Stephen Sondheim. *Maddie* was chosen as the basis of the third programme in the series and Keeling and McKenna were invited to participate. Four songs from the show were recorded - by Rognlie, Colson, Richards and Vincent Leigh, who was front-runner to play Nick in the West End, McGann having already committed to a leading role in a major television series, *The Grand.*

Sondheim was charming, friendly and encouraging. Though the writers were extremely nervous - knowing how critical Sondheim could be - the interview turned out to be highly enjoyable. Best of all was that the broadcast date was set to be immediately before the West End opening in March, and reference was made to this in the interview.

[The entire programme can now be heard online at https://soundcloud.com/stephen-keeling-1/in-company-with-sondheim-maddie. SMcK]

Maddie would be the first of the shows workshopped by Sondheim at Oxford to make it to the West End.

Weeks had gone by and Wax was becoming concerned that he had not received a signed contract from Apollo Leisure - as did Stephen Waley-Cohen at the Vaudeville, who was concerned about how he could fill his theatre should the deal fall through. Wax repeatedly called Adrian Leggatt and, when he finally reached him, was promised that the contract would be biked to Wax's office by noon the following day. It never arrived.

Verbal commitments continued to be made. Although perhaps the writing was on the wall, Wax was reassured that Apollo would progress, as he had already made Summer Rognlie a formal offer to repeat her performance as Maddie. Finally a signature date was agreed and the parties met at the Victoria Palace. Leggatt apologised profusely and explained that Apollo Leisure had no choice but to pull out. Wax appreciated that Leggatt found himself in a very embarrassing position and was genuinely distressed by the news he was forced to bring.

Wax and Waley-Cohen faced big problems. Waley-Cohen had a

theatre to fill (in fact, the Vaudeville remained dark for several weeks) and Wax had to find something in the region of 180,000. More importantly, Wax had given his word to a large number of people that the show was about to happen. Now the carpet had been pulled away from under him.

On the strength of *Maddie*'s imminent West End production, Summer Rognlie had turned down a contract at the National Theatre to play a supporting role and understudy Maria Friedman in *Lady In The Dark*. Wax immediately called Rognlie's agent, Jane Wynn-Owen, and told her she had better accept the National Theatre job. Wynn-Owen generously said that she thought she could keep the offer on hold for a further week, while the creative team contacted everyone they could possibly think of to try to raise the shortfall. But it was not to be - and Rognlie went to the National on a contract that lasted until the end of July 1997.

The day that Wax had to sit down and call every one of the *Maddie* team with the news was one of the worst days of his life. He felt physically sick each time he picked up the phone. What got him through it was the response of the entire creative team, and the cast. They were entirely sympathetic to Wax's position, reassured him that he *would* get the show on somewhere, somehow and that they would continue to support him. McKenna, Dexter and Keeling even offered to put their eventual advance against royalties into the show if it was the only way to get it on.

Over the next few weeks, battered and bruised but bouncing back determinedly, Wax continued to approach potential investors to persuade them to part with some money. He had an appointment with someone at the Really Useful Group who was very supportive of Wax personally and said that he would pass the script, tape and reviews package on to the relevant people in the company - who would decide whether or not they could support the show. Wax was up-front. He said he was looking for a co-producer but, to be honest, would be happy with even a small investment. He didn't expect people to put a lot of money in - but hoped that a lot of people would invest a little bit of money. Wax felt he might be in with a chance as, at around this time, articles were appearing in the press from leading producers, saying that new talent must be encouraged or the next generation of musicals would be unable to emerge.

Wax finally received a letter from the Really Useful Company's managing director, James Thane, saying that he thought the script was sensational and the songs were wonderful but, unfortunately, it was not the company's policy to invest in shows in which they would not be the lead producer. Wax was deeply disappointed that they were not even prepared to buy a single unit of 1,000.

Everywhere he went, it seemed, Wax was hitting brick walls.

The Radio 2 broadcast, *In Company With Sondheim*, had to be tagged with an additional comment that a major backer of the West End production had pulled out and that the opening was postponed. The BBC failed to include this comment when a section of the show was repeated on Radio 4's *Pick of the Week* and a number of people phoned the theatre, only to be told that the show would not be playing there.

In February 1997, *Lady In The Dark* opened at the National Theatre. On the day of the press night, one of Rognlie's friends had to cancel her ticket. Rognlie invited Wax. The cast had clubbed together for a big opening gala dinner and when, she met him there, he had some interesting news.

During the interval, the *Telegraph* critic, Charles Spencer was pointed out to him. Wax had never met Spencer but decided he had nothing to lose by introducing himself.

'My name is Kenny Wax,' he said. 'You don't know me at all, but I was the producer of *Maddie* at the Salisbury Playhouse and we were very grateful for your review. I wondered whether you'd like to know why we haven't transferred, after such a good collection of reviews.' He told Spencer the story.

Spencer wondered at first whether he had been over-enthusiastic in his original review. Wax sent him a copy of the Sondheim interview and Spencer phoned up a few days later to say that he really did like the show. Wax sent him some further information.

The following Saturday, a large colour photograph and piece appeared in Spencer's Arts Notebook in the *Telegraph*:

> Who'd be an eager young producer of British musicals? In a West End dominated by Lord Lloyd-Webber, Boublil and Schonberg, and endless revivals, it seems almost impossible for newcomers to break into the big time.
>
> Last September, I travelled to Salisbury to see that rare creature, a new British musical by unknown writers. It was called *Maddie* and it was terrific, a tale of Hollywood ambition and ghostly possession that was funny, touching and blessed with a wonderful star performance from Summer Rognlie, an actress-singer in the Liza Minnelli mould.
>
> Theatrical bigshots hustled down to Salisbury to catch the production but, six months on, it has still to arrive in the West End.
>
> The young producer, Kenny Wax, explained some of the problems to me. The show was within an ace of

transferring, a theatre was lined up but his powerful co-producers pulled out just before contracts were signed.

And, although Lord Lloyd-Webber has frettted about the absence of young talent in British musical theatre and complained of 'working in a vacuum', his own Really Useful Company recently refused to cough up a measly 1,000 for *Maddie*, even though its managing director James Thane said he 'really enjoyed listening to the songs' and thought the book was 'sensational.'

Apparently, the Really Useful Company becomes involved only if it takes a 'lead production role', but surely it could useful dish out a fraction of its profits to provide initial finance for exciting new projects without necessarily becoming the main producer.

Wax has done his homework and reckons there hasn't been a single new musical by a British composer in the West End for five years - with the exception of those written by Lloyd Webber.

'There is very little support from the industry for young writers and young producers, which is a great pity. Those who have helped me can be counted on the fingers of one hand. If there are so few new shows now, what will we be reviving in fifteen years time?'

However, Wax refuses to give up, and is determined to present *Maddie* in the West End. There's also big interest in America, Australia and Scandinavia, but he has to open in London first. The budget is an exceptionally modest 340,000 and Wax is 150,000 short of the total.

> I have to say that becoming a theatrical 'angel' is a notoriously risky business, but if you are interested in becoming involved in a show of real heart and promise, investment is available in units of 1,000. Wax can be contacted at...(here he included Wax's address)
>
> It would be gratifying if Lord Lloyd-Webber were among the first to send a cheque. If professional etiquette didn't forbid it, I'd take a gamble on this hugely engaging show myself.

Wax phoned Spencer to thank him for this tremendous boost, and went away on a week's much-needed ski-ing break. He came back to find a foot-high pile of letters from people whose hearts had been touched by this story. Some extracts establish the tone:

> ... I am 70 years old, have never done, nor contemplated doing such a thing before – it's a case of a new cooker or a gamble, and I don't do the lottery...
>
> ...This week I received an unexpected windfall from the tax man, of all people. Having read Charles Spencer's account of your *Maddie* ambition, I have decided to enjoy my good fortune by investing in your project. Hopefully there are another 149 like me...
>
> ...I don't always agree with Charles Spencer's reviews but my imagination has been caught by his article...
>
> ... As an 83 year old pensioner I am not normally in a position to gamble, but I value Charles Spencer as my theatre critic whose judgement has always been correct and his report... has fired my imagination...
>
> ... Though I've never done anything of this kind be-

> fore - but then, theologically, I suppose all angels are virgins, I'd like a grand's worth of the action... Realistically I don't have much expectation of seeing my money again, but when they asked Hugo Gryn if he believed in life after death, he replied, 'I'm ready for pleasant surprises.'

Wax immediately sent prospectuses off to the eighty people who had expressed interest. Cheques started to arrive by return of post.

◆ ◆ ◆

In March, still short of funding, Wax decided to go to America. He bought a plane ticket, stayed with a friend in New York and, keeping the expedition as cheap as he possibly could, he determined to bring *Maddie* to the attention of American producers. *Maddie* was, after all, a story set in America, in the great Broadway tradition. Wax did not know whether this trip would be a complete waste of time or not but he thought, 'If you don't have a go, you'll never know.'

He ended up having a very busy week, meeting lots of producers, including some of the biggest names on Broadway. Some turned him down flat, some expressed interest. Lee Menzies, an established West End figure who was thinking about joining the project as a co-producer, provided one very productive introduction. This was to Barry Brown, who had been one of the producers of both the Angela Lansbury and Tyne Daly revivals of *Gypsy* on Broadway, as well as *La Cage Aux Folles* (Jerry Herman's Broadway smash hit). The day after Wax returned to England, Brown faxed him and declared himself eager to be involved.

Brown recalls:

> Lee Menzies and I have known each other since 1971

> and he called me one day to say this young producer was coming to New York. Kenny arrived, we had lunch at Joe Allen's and he gave me a script. Kenny reminded me of me twenty five years ago - dauntless and fearless and determined to march forward at any expense. That 'It has to work because I'm going to make it work' attitude. I read the script that night, liked it - it has an emotional and psychological blending and it really makes you care - and said, 'OK, I'm prepared to be a part of this.' It was that straightforward. I had no problems raising the money - around 85,000. It took four or five phone calls and it took no more than a day.

The ease with which Brown raised the money was partly due to his excellent track record, particularly over the last ten or twelve years.

Brown continues:

> Steve Sondheim and I are good friends. After I became involved, I saw him and told him that I was going over to London and why. He said, 'Oh my God! Things go full circle, don't they? He was thrilled that I was involved.

He and Wax did a deal whereby Brown acquired the US rights, and his investment was promised and delivered. Wax was naturally thrilled, particularly as the American market is both right and potentially hugely profitable for *Maddie*.

As Tim Rice wrote in *Evita,* 'the money kept rolling in.'

◆ ◆ ◆

There were some moments during the money-raising process

which were amusing, others which were nail-bitingly tense. Wax recalls one potential investor, a woman in her sixties, who was very secretive about her potential involvement. Wax had to telephone her at specific times so that her husband would not find out what she was planning. Finally, she invited him to her home. She asked a few bizarre and random questions and then, quite out of the blue, told Wax that she had always felt she could have been a professional singer. Would he indulge her by listening to her tape? Out of politeness, Wax agreed to hear one song. Several songs later, amid many apologies that the tape was made without her usual accompanist, she asked, 'Could I have made it? Could I have been a star?' Wax was as non-committal as possible and made a hurried escape. Needless to say, he declined her investment.

One Sunday lunchtime, a mother and son came to Wax's flat. Wax expected a half hour meeting but found himself having to play the tape, explain the songs and the staging in detail and every nuance of the characters. The son was about nineteen and clearly considered himself God's gift to musical theatre. He wanted to take away a script to read. Wax refused, saying that the boy could sit in the office and read the script if he wanted but, for the sake of confidentiality, scripts were not available to the general public. The boy, like certain other potential investors, started to make suggestions about things that did and did not work in the script, without having either seen *Maddie* or read it. They did not invest either.

Fortunately, some meetings were of more practical use. One man, who had seen the show in Salisbury and invested two thousand pounds, invited Wax to have dinner with his son, a merchant banker. By the end of the meal, Wax went away with a guarantee of a further twenty three thousand pounds, actually clutching a cheque for ten thousand.

◆ ◆ ◆

A few weeks later, Spencer wrote a follow-up piece:

> Readers of *Arts and Books* are angels - and that's official. A few weeks ago, I reported on the plight of the young producer, Kenny Wax, who had been left in the lurch by his co-producers and was struggling to find the cash to transfer the new musical, *Maddie*, to the West End.
>
> Wax was overwhelmed by your response. He received 80 letters from *Telegraph* readers, of whom 40 subsequently came up with the readies, investing a total of 75,000 in the show. If you want to get on board now, you'll need to hurry. From being 150,000 down, Wax now needs only between 25,000 and 50,000 to get the show on in a West End theatre in the autumn. He can be contacted at... (address).
>
> My only worry now is that the show - a funny, touching tale of ghostly goings on in Hollywood with a sensational star performance from Summer Rognlie - will prove as successful in the West End as it did at its Salisbury tryout.
>
> I must repeat my original warning: theatrical investment is notoriously risky, but, if you've got a grand of 'fun' money, you'll be investing it in a show of real promise and heart.

This led to further commitments from people who had written the first time, plus new *Telegraph* readers ready to put their money where Spencer's mouth was. In all, Wax received around 120 letters and raised around 150,000, the crucial middle chunk. The generosity of Spencer and his readers made the show possible. His piece created a knock-on enthusiasm which greatly aided Wax in achieving the full capitalisation. Spencer did what he did, not for Wax or McKenna or Dexter or Keeling, but for the theatre and the general public. He believed that *Maddie* should have her chance to be a star. There was, of course, no guarantee that his review of the final production would be good.

◆ ◆ ◆

Maddie's determination to be a star seemed, once more, to be spilling over from fiction to fact. Yet again, the show had seemed a dead duck. Yet again, through an almost-miraculous chain of events, *Maddie* had come back to life.

Lee Menzies came on board as co-producer and now he and Wax set about their search for the right theatre. Some larger houses were on offer but Wax stuck to his guns about finding an appropriately sized venue, with an auditorium that felt intimate but allowed the possibility of the show meeting its financial commitments. A September/October opening was planned and for a while it looked as though a suitable venue might not be available -which would have pushed the opening back to Spring 1998, eighteen months after Salisbury.

The theatre negotiations were very tense. Wax describes it as:

> like playing poker, because you never know who else they are negotiating with. I'd already turned down the Aldwych because it was too big. We were still pursuing Stephen Waley-Cohen for the Vaudeville, because he had been prepared to make a very favourable deal, but he had plans for a comedy season and would not commit to *Maddie* - even though I kept sending him deposit cheques. The Lyric, Shaftesbury

> Avenue - a Stoll-Moss house - had been pencilled in for Cameron Mackintosh's *The Fix*, which had been expected to transfer from the Donmar Warehouse. However, after a poor critical reception, the West End transfer was cancelled. The Lyric, which is in the heart of the West End and visible from Piccadilly Circus, seats 660 and was ideal for *Maddie*. We knew that other people wanted the theatre - *Popcorn* was doing good business at the Apollo next door, which always helps in terms of passing trade.

Ultimately, Menzies and Wax formalised a deal with Stoll Moss to open at the Lyric on September 22nd 1997. The investors, the writers and the co-producers were delighted at the choice of theatre. Contracts were signed.
This time around, even though the creative team were hugely relieved and excited, champagne bottles were not opened. Once bitten...

But there was no need to be twice shy. *Maddie* was definitely, finally about to happen. McKenna, when he heard, burst into tears.

MADDIE, DANCING

Well, she got her break...

Rognlie's contract at the National Theatre ended on July 30th 1997 and rehearsals for *Maddie* began three weeks later. It worked out perfectly. Wax, Connor and the team had discussed what would happen if Rognlie should prove unavailable, and everyone agreed that she was so sensational that *Maddie* was now unimaginable without her.

McKenna recalls:

> I felt strongly that Summer would quickly be recognised as a major star. We had written a potentially star-making role, as Streisand had in *Funny Girl* - the 'marriage' of Maddie and Summer could not be more perfect. If *Maddie* made Summer a star, that would also be good for the show.

Kevin Colson was committed to the 1997 season at the Chichester Festival Theatre where he was appearing in *Divorce Me, Darling* with Ruthie Henshall and Liliane Montevecchi. The dates of his final performances clashed with the previews and first week of *Maddie*. For a time it looked as though Colson, whose performance was central, would be lost - but Wax managed to negotiate a contract buy-out for the last two weeks which enabled Colson to rehearse during the day, travel down to Chichester for his show, and play all the previews as well as the all-important first night.

The team were sad to lose Angela Richards as Mrs van Arc. She had accepted a role in *Enter The Guardsman* at the Donmar Warehouse, which opened two weeks before *Maddie*. Richards had made the rich widow her own but the team were delighted when Lynda Baron agreed to play it. Lynda had been discussed when the Salisbury production was being cast and, for McKenna, had stolen the West End revival of *Little Me* from under the noses of Russ Abbott and Sheila White. Baron was voluptuous, classy and sexy, with a great singing voice. She was also very, very funny - perfect for Mrs van Arc.

Graham Bickley was cast as Nick. He recalls:

> Kenny was keeping an eye on the whole Disney fallout, and eventually contacted me and offered me the role of Nick. There would be no dressing room redecoration, no TV, certainly no driver, but I was very happy to accept.

Wax wanted to include as many of the Salisbury cast as possible. However, the role of Sally had been written out and there was really nothing suitable to offer Yvonne Edgell. Hattie Ladbury had played the ghost of Maddie but this was now a dancing role and Hattie was not a dancer. Daniel Coll and David Credell were both unavailable. Beth Tuckey was once again cast as Mrs Klein - now with a more substantial role - and Jon Rumney was delighted to reprise his comic waiter and exasperated security guard. It was also pleasing to be able to cast another of the *Maddie* family, Russell Wilcox, as Hugo Dahl. Wilcox had played Nick in the Manchester and London showcases. Other new members of the company were Paddy Glynn, Nicola Filshie, Louise Davidson and Michael Elliott. Casting was completed with barely a fortnight before full company rehearsals began - with the exception of Martin Parr, cast as Young Al, who was finally offered the role with just three days' notice.

The process of casting understudies who also play minor roles is surprisingly difficult. Naturally, they need to have the talent and expertise to play the major roles in event of a star's illness, but they also have to be perfect for the roles they play in their own right. Finding a sufficiently tall male dancer, for example, who could believably grow up to be the very masculine Kevin Colson, was surprisingly tough.

◆ ◆ ◆

There was just one more set of rewrites. Earlier in the year, Warner-Chappell had asked for a tape of the complete score, which they needed for administration and publicity purposes. Rognlie, Richards and Colson recorded their roles and John Barr made a splendid Nick.

However, it was this recording that threw up a problem with the new song, *Don't Look Back.* Rognlie felt that it was too much to expect of her to sing this very demanding duet immediately prior to going into *Star,* if she was going to be able to do the latter justice. Wax also had reservations about the structure of the song, though everyone loved the melody and the passion of it.

Keeling rewrote the middle section and sent it to McKenna to set. He suggested that Jan should not sing the final section - that it should be largely a number for Nick. McKenna then had a long telephone conversation with Dexter, because Keeling's suggestion created a problem. If Nick was singing alone, all he could really say was 'Don't leave me!' There is already a 'Don't leave me' song in Act Two - *Afraid.* This was not the right place in the show to express this sentiment, or *Afraid* would go for nothing.

Dexter and McKenna batted it back and forth for an hour or so. It had already been planned that *Don't Look Back* would recur during the show, with extracts in Scene One for Nick and Jan and as the Finale. The pair finally had a brainwave and, coincidentally, solved a problem which had bugged *Maddie* since its inception. The song, in a lighter arrangement and a jokey, quasi-romantic mood, would appear in its entirety in Scene One. A truncated duet version would then appear before *Star* and an almost full version reprise at the Finale. This meant that *Don't Look Back* effectively became the elusive opening number for Nick and Jan, established Keeling's theme strongly as 'their tune' and brought the piece to a rousing romantic conclusion. As everything else slotted into place, it seemed fitting that the last piece of the jigsaw should be the opening number - and a good omen that it was entitled *Don't Look Back*.

When Caroline Humphris came to think about the orchestrations for the West End production, of which she would also be musical director (due to the unavailability of Martin Lowe), she decided to cut the cello. There had been problems with the sound at Salisbury and, although Humphris had been very happy with the use of the cello in the BBC recording for *In Company With Sondheim*, it remained a difficult instrument to amplify. She felt it was too much of a risk. She decided to add a trumpet and a second keyboard. The second keyboard would add texture and fill out the middle of the arrangements while the trumpet added a very Broadway 'brass' sound. There were now to be no strings at all in the arrangements - faced with a budget-induced choice, Humphris was marshalling her resources carefully. There were string sounds on the keyboard but these had to be used discreetly and sparingly as electronic sounds can sometimes jar with those of acoustic instruments. The second keyboard was also used to supplement the brass. Humphris went even further with the jazz feel of the orchestrations - the addition of a trumpet was a great help in this regard. The three wind instruments also enabled her to write some Andrews Sisters-type harmonies.

Humphris had some doubts about taking on her dual role as orchestrator/MD at first, because of the physical and mental toll the Salisbury process had taken on her. However, she decided that she knew the piece very well and the original orchestrations now existed as a basis for her work. There was one advantage - there would no longer be a need to mediate between the orchestrator, MD and composer. Now she could see what was happening in rehearsal and go home and put it down on paper.

She also had to organise the music into its various incarnations for different purposes - rehearsal score, the complete orchestral arrangement, band parts etc - a logistical nightmare in which she had to second-guess everything that might happen.

Niki Turner, too, had some re-thinking to do in terms of design. A move to a proscenium-arch theatre had always been behind her design concept and she now had a little more money to spend - though the budget was eaten into by the fact that in Salisbury she had been able to utilise the Playhouse's own blacks and gauzes, whereas West End productions have to provide their own. An early meeting had suggested that the apartment set, in which so much of the action takes place, needed to be more three dimensional and warmer in colour. It was also suggested that the party be set on the terrace of Mrs van Arc's mansion, rather than inside, to provide greater visual variety.

Turner had been pleased with the overall effect at Salisbury, especially the use of light boxes for the San Francisco skyline and Mrs van Arc's mansion in the distance. Because of the shape of the Salisbury stage, however, she felt that too much had been seen of the blacks - she had conceived the design as objects in space rather than objects against a black background. This, she felt sure, would work better in a proscenium arch theatre, where the lighting could be really focussed on the key elements. The lighting designer, Brian 'Basher' Harris, was delighted with the challenge of objects in space and the two worked together to create a magic box effect. More light was built into the set itself.

The Lyric was also a better space than the Vaudeville, the proposed first venue for a transfer, which has minimal wing space. The cinema could now be built on a truck, to spin round, whereas it would have had to be flown - and the change from outside to inside would have been more complicated.

Some sections of the Salisbury set had been damaged in storage, when a pigeon got into the store-room and messed all over the van Arc mansion set. However, as with the script, the concept remained basically unchanged - it was a question of adding polish.

◆ ◆ ◆

Shortly before rehearsals began, Wax was surprised and delighted to receive a letter from Jack Finney's widow, Margaret, enclosing a cheque for one thousand pounds:

> It gives my family and me great pleasure to know that people are still so interested in Jack's work. I admire your perseverance in bringing *Maddie* to life. If my involvement (limited though it may be) in your production can be any use to you for further publicity, please do not hesitate to milk it for all it is worth.

◆ ◆ ◆

Rehearsals began for the principals on August 26th, at the National Folk Song and Dance Society, Regents Park. The remainder of the company joined a week later, on September 1st. Before the read-through on that day, Connor spoke eloquently about the underlying themes and concepts he found in the show:

> I've always felt that *Maddie* can be enjoyed on many levels - it's funny, witty, interesting, entertaining, magical, the music's great... Children could quite happily enjoy it - the story is surprising and compelling. It's a good yarn. But there's also a more resonant

side to it. If you want to think about what the show explores, as well as just experience it, it poses questions.

Maddie is an earthbound spirit, trapped because she cannot let go. Jan and Nick are also trapped - their marriage cannot grow because they themselves have never really grown. There's a Russian philosopher, George Gurdjieff, who says, 'If you want to escape from prison, the first thing you must realise is that you are in prison. If you think you are free, no escape is possible.' That's exactly Nick and Jan's predicament. They're stuck because they haven't opened their hearts to each other, but they don't realise that.

Most of us are frightened of opening our hearts because it makes us feel vulnerable. But *who* is frightened? What is our identity? How do we define ourselves? When we fall in love with someone, do we fall in love with a body, a personality, a soul, a combination of all three - or *only* a combination of all three?

People who believe that just the physical body is at the centre of their lives get very concerned about growing older, for as they start to lose their beauty or their faculties they start to panic. People who think their personality defines them spend much of their time making statements, 'I do this. I'm this sort of person.' Some people identify with the soul, the thing that sits behind the personality as though it is a spirit which has taken form in this particular body and which, starting in infancy, has learned to take on the personality.

Most of us identify more strongly with one of these aspects of life than with the others. Mostly, it's the personality. But our reality is constantly dissolving and what we think is permanent proves temporary. A Tibetan lama named Kalu Rinpoche says, 'We live in illusion, the appearance of things. But there is a reality - we are that reality. When you understand that, you see that you are nothing and, being nothing, are everything. That is all there is.'

Now, all this may sound very abstruse and intellectual when talking about a musical comedy, but it does have relevance to *Maddie*.

Maddie thought she lived life to the full, and in a way she did. Though she lives for the moment, her ambition and determination result in her death. In death, that ambition and determination are transformed into an overwhelming longing, which blinds her. When she comes back, in the action of the play, the events lead her to understand that while it is right to live in the moment - because that is ultimately all any of us have - she needs to live in the *complete* moment, which does not just involve her but those around her. Living in 'the moment' with mindfulness means appreciating not only one's own narrow concerns but all the happiness, joy, despair and sadness that exist in that moment. At the end, when Maddie gets the role, she learns that the very thing she has been clinging to is what has caused her to be stuck and unhappy. Her need dissolves. Stardom was driving her on and was hugely meaningful to her. Now it seems unimportant. She has nothing more to prove. She appreciates Al, Nick and Jan for what they are - and herself for what she is - and that makes her free.

The same process can be seen with Nick and Jan. The disruption Maddie causes to their lives makes them question everything and break out of the narrow confines they have built for themselves and each other. They can start again, afresh, with knowledge.

At the end of the first week of rehearsals, the tragic news hit the world of the death of Diana, Princess of Wales in a car crash. Apart from the shock and sense of loss that the company shared with the rest of the country, there was immediate concern about the car crashes in the show. Maddie dies in a car crash on the way to Hollywood in 1926, and there was a second crash during Maddie's journey to Hollywood in Act Two. Would this press the wrong buttons, hit a wrong nerve, seem in bad taste?

The second car crash was cut - not entirely because of Princess Diana's tragic death. It had always seemed to worry the audience - they thought fate was repeating itself and Maddie was dying before she got her big chance. It was decided, however, to keep Maddie's death in the 1926 car crash. It seemed important to establish that Maddie had died because of her own nature. This had no echoes in Princess Diana's tragedy.

Graham Bickley, Kevin Colson and Summer Rognlie

Rehearsals went smoothly and steadily. The work undertaken on the show since Salisbury held up well and only minor nips and tucks were necessary. Connor concentrated on ensuring that all the characters - from Jan to the party guests - were grounded in naturalistic reality. Jenny Arnold, standing in for an indisposed David Toguri worked from this basis in the staged and choreographed sequences. *[David was more than indisposed. Not long afterwards, this great man of the theatre and delightful companion, passed away. SMcK]* Except in one or two dance sequences, the movement was a shaped and heightened form of naturalism.

Rognlie and Colson had played *Maddie* before, of course. If Graham Bickley and Lynda Baron found this inhibiting, they did not show it. Jan had been slightly redefined as a character, and Rognlie and Bickley effectively had a different relationship to explore from that of Rognlie and McGann. Bickley soon found moments of great comedy in Nick and for the first time the emotional ending of the show was the reconciliation of the pair, not the final departure of Maddie. Baron spent many rehearsals just watching Rognlie play the Maddie scenes, so that her own interpretation of the long-dead flapper could be recognisably the same character. She used Rognlie's 'Maddie movements' to excellent effect. Her Mrs van Arc, too, was no mere vamp but a three dimensional character who behaved badly but whom one could not help liking.

Another odd piece of news occurred in the second week of rehearsals. Jenny Gould, one of Wax's assistants, received a phone call from her parents, who were holidaying in Italy. They had stopped in Assisi, in the square in front of the Basilica Santa Chiara. On one side of the square was a hundred feet long stone wall topped with iron lattice work, beyond whch could be seen a magnificent view. When Gould's father went to sit down, facing him was some graffiti, painted in white on the stone wall. It read, 'Maddie!

Graham Bickley and Summer Rognlie

Barry Brown came over from New York during rehearsals to play a hands-on role in the production. His incisiveness and eye for detail reminded the writers of Sondheim. Of his active participation, Brown says:

> I wouldn't do it any other way. I'm not a money raiser, I'm a producer. In fact, my strength as a producer is working with the creative team and developing material. That's what I'm best at and, consequently, what I enjoy most. It's exciting for me, too, working on something new.
>
> For the last three years I have been working on a tour of *West Side Story* - which is great - but there's always a buzz about something new.
>
> The subject matter of *Maddie* - life after death and spirituality - feels very timely to me. And it's, in the best sense of the word, an old-fashioned musical, pre-chandeliers and helicopters. I think that's what the theatre has to go back to. It'll take ten steps forward by going back to that.

◆ ◆ ◆

The previous show at the Lyric, *Marlene*, closed on September 5th. During the course of the next week, the auditorium and foyers were repainted and new carpets laid. This was an extra benefit - *Maddie* would be re-opening a smart, re-furbished theatre.

Steven Dexter and Kenny Wax the day the first poster went up outside the Lyric

The technical team, overseen by production manager Paul O'Leary, installed the revolve and the flats and the lighting was hung, ready for technical rehearsals starting on the evening of September 17th.

September 17th arrived but *Maddie* was in no position to begin a technical rehearsal. Some of the scenery had yet to arrive, some had yet to be hung and there were key elements (including the ghost effect) which were not yet ready. When the full set is not prepared it obviously causes the lighting designer considerable difficulties, particularly with lighting effects that have been built into pieces of scenery. The delay in the build caused a knock-on delay with focusing and angling the lights and when the technical rehearsal began on the morning of September

18th, the going was very slow indeed.

However, the first band call that evening lifted everyone's spirits. This was the first time the writers and the company had heard Caroline Humphris' new orchestrations. They were very exciting, with energy, a great Broadway sound and tremendous detail. Graham Bickley bought champagne for everyone, Lee Menzies bought more and there was a real party atmosphere in the stalls bar, where the band was playing.

Kenny Wax at the band call

Meanwhile, in the auditorium, matters technical were still proceeding at a snail's pace.

The first preview was scheduled for Monday 22nd, with scheduled dress rehearsals on the preceding Saturday night and Monday afternoon. The technical rehearsal finally reached the end of the show at 6pm on the Saturday, though because of the absence of key scenic elements, some sections of the show had barely been touched.

A technical/dress rehearsal began at 8pm that evening. The first act took nearly two hours and only the first two scenes of the second act could be attempted before the end of the call for performers and band. The company were beginning to get extremely agitated - the whole thing was very behind. There was a general feeling among the creative team that Wax would have no choice but to cancel the first preview - a decision Wax resisted for as long as he could (the preview being sold out) before acknowledging that he had little other choice.

Rognlie recalls:

> "I'll never forget when we were about to start public previews for Maddie on the West End. It had become a technical challenge, to say the least; there were so many more complicated levels to the West End's production. We hadn't finished tech rehearsals for the show, and an audience was due in that night. I was going to have to go out on stage blind for the second half of the show with no idea of what would happen. I remember knowing the tech wasn't ready to be shown to an audience. There was so much buzz and hype surrounding the opening, and all I could think was that if we went on before we were ready, it would be a disaster! This show meant too much to all of us for that to happen. The entire creative team gathered in Graham Bickley's dressing room to decide what to do. I remember I was just sobbing, devastated at the thought of performing in front of an audience without being ready. But canceling a preview would have had its own repercussions. So very much at stake. I remember our director, Martin Conner, with such a calm presence in the room while we formu-

> lated what to do. He listened and quietly contemplated the best course of action. We all sat there in silence, waiting, until Martin nodded his head and stood up—and that was that.
>
> We decided to cancel the preview and finish the tech rehearsal that evening instead. It was all very emotional and dramatic, but I think everyone was secretly relieved that we waited.

The dress rehearsal on Monday 22nd September went well, though there were still problems with scene changes, set dressing was virtually non-existent and one or two scenic elements were still missing. However, the company pulled together with tremendous energy and commitment and everyone went home feeling, 'We have a show.'

Rognlie recalls:

> When we did open for previews the next evening and the show went well, the producer, Kenny Wax said, "See, it would have all been fine!" I replied, "it was fine BECAUSE we cancelled and finished the tech for the show." I love that we all stood together when making that very tough decision. We were all so invested, both in each other and in the show's success. That deep support and admiration we felt for each other is something I'll never forget."

Over the next few days, throughout the first previews, most of Rognlie's costumes were replaced.

In the run-up to the first performances, some of the key players were asked how they felt.

Kevin Colson:

> Success is not a right, nor a foregone conclusion. But if *Maddie* succeeds, it will be just reward for all those

who made it possible. As for me? Old George in *Aspects of Love* used to say - 'Life goes on... love goes free.' Selfishly, I want *Maddie* to run forever because I love the role of Al and cherish moments such as when I sing *Maddie, Dancing* and a tear rolls down the cheek of David Toguri - or when I speak my final line (thrown in as a 'filler' to get me off the stage) and the author stifles a sob. Magic!

Shaun McKenna:

It's the first West End show for a lot of us. That's incredibly exciting and somewhat daunting. I'm trying to enjoy the *process* of what's happening and not to concentrate on the outcome. Of course, if *Maddie* is a hit - and I can't believe it won't be - my life could change drastically as a result. Quite apart from some very welcome income, it could lead to many, many possibilities. If it's a flop, perhaps nobody will ever employ me again. But most importantly, I've come to see how much of me there is in the book and lyrics, and how passionately I believe in the message of the show. I feel as if I'm offering my heart on a plate - it's a big risk. But I think there are enough people out there to give Madeline Marsh - who is now utterly real to me - the credit she deserves.

Kenny Wax:

At the end of the day, I'm Joe Public and I love showbiz and watching people being entertained. If *Maddie* doesn't run in the West End, then we will have given it our very best shot. If it flops, probably there isn't a career for me in producing. I've spent nine years working my way up to this point, the last three years on *Maddie*, because I passionately believe that this is a show that people will enjoy and that critics should, on the whole, like. You can't expect unanimous critical praise - that would be unrealistic. But if audiences don't get excited by this show, then this isn't the career for me. The last few months have been the most enjoyable and exciting months of my life, seeing *Maddie* come towards the West End - and I just hope and pray that people will love the show as we love it. It has been written, performed and produced with so much love and so much care - with respect for each other, our cast and our crew... It was written from the soul and it's been produced from the soul. Let's have a hit!

Barry Brown:

We're all here for one reason, much as we like theatre and the sense that we're going to create something that will last... Lily Tomlin once said, 'They don't call it show-art, they call it showbusiness.' It's how I pay my rent. If I don't have a show running, I don't have an income. So I want *Maddie* to enjoy a long and successful run and see it on Broadway in eighteen months.

THERE WE WERE

At opening night on September 29th 1997, the three writers took their seats in the middle of an auditorium crammed with investors, friends – and critics. Stomachs churned, shoulders were tense. Loved ones held hands and murmured encouragement.

At the first scene change, as the revolve turned, the incoming backdrop clipped the table on the apartment set with a sickening thud. That was enough for McKenna, who made a beeline for the exit. He found Dexter in the Stalls Bar and not long afterwards Keeling joined them. They listened to the show – and the audience reaction – on the front of house tannoy.

Families and friends were as positive as only families and friends can be and by the time everyone headed off to Imagination, where Kenny Wax had organised an excellent first night party, the team had reason to think that it might – just might - all have gone well. The reception from the investors at the party was warm and encouraging and, as at every first night party there has ever been, the evening swam along on a wave of euphoria and optimism.

There had been a concern that with one critic, Charles Spencer, having thrown his weight behind the show it might have irritated his colleagues on other papers. One rival critic, who shall be nameless, had recently had a book of his reviewed harshly by Spencer and there were rumours of a feud. There was talk that *Maddie* might end being caught in the crossfire, the show being used to "demonstrate" Spencer's "lack of judgement." Was that true? Who knows?

McKenna heard the thud of the newspaper landing on his doormat early next morning and ran downstairs to see what Michael Coveney had written in the *Daily Mail* – traditionally the first review out. The review was prominently placed on page three. The headline read, "*Maddie* is a baddie – and a soppy one at that." It was like being punched in the stomach.

The other nationals had not yet published. The next one expected was that day's *Evening Standard* and the much-feared (and now largely forgotten) Nicholas de Jongh. De Jongh rarely liked anything. By mid morning, we knew that the Standard review was a stinker too. "Balderdash, babble and baloney leading to a dead end... It's a grim night." There were three crucial newspapers whose reviews carried weight in 1997 – *The Mail* and the *Standard* were two of them.

Deeply thrown, McKenna and his wife took their dogs for a long, silent walk in Richmond Park. It was a foggy morning and the fog seemed symbolic – it was difficult to see a way forward.

The company had been called for five o'clock. Everyone put on their bravest faces. Kenny Wax and Martin Connor both spoke to the company and were encouraging and inspirational. We all made much of the legendary shows that had been slaughtered by the critics and went on to be enormous hits. We came out of the company call heartened. It was only two reviews. Perhaps the rest would be better. Meanwhile, we had a show to do.

The rest of the reviews came in over the next few days and, sure enough, a lot of them were better. The national Sunday papers received "Maddie" considerably more positively than the dailies. We ended up with almost half of the reviews ranging from good to excellent.

Kate Bassett in the Daily Telegraph wrote:

> "Startlingly confident, offering Broadway-style numbers and evocatively echoing tunes from the jazz age... Shaun McKenna and Steven Dexter's book manages multiple lot twists commendably and Martin Connor's cast are delightfully assured. Lynda Baron is splendid as an art collector's widow and mighty-voiced Rognlie is clearly a star in the making."

Michael Billington in the Guardian wrote:

> "The book, by Shaun McKenna and Steven Dexter keeps the plot spinning and Stephen Keeling's music switches neatly between periods..."

Irving Wardle in the Sunday Telegraph said:

> "Some dizzily inventive scenes ... Music propels

this well-carpentered fairy tale into another dimension. See-sawing between dreamy lyricism and driving asymmetrical rhythms, Keeling's score... does all that's needed to lift the story into a magical zone where the living can join hands with the dead and romance cohabit with bedroom farce. In McKenna's lyrics, as in the score, Sondheim rubs shoulders with Jerome Kern."

John Peter in the Sunday Times, commenting on the show's move from Salisbury, wrote:

"It has kept its haunting, oddball, slightly mad charm and its touching mixture of the real and the improbable, of wisdom and innocence... The book and lyrics are perky and witty... Warmly recommended."

The Mail on Sunday wrote:

"I'm in two minds about *Maddie.* I know it's got something going for it but I'm not sure it's enough."

Unfortunately, slightly more than half the reviews were negative. These varied from Benedict Nightingale's measured but generally unfavourable *Times* review:

"Composer Stephen Keeling and librettists Shaun McKenna and Steven Dexter embrace few of the opportunities open to them. They have created a pleasant little musical with some agreeable hums between some diverting chatter but for my money the sophistication level is a bit too low and the sentimentality rate rather too high."

To some really savage comments –

"For the most part it's not what possesses its heroine that preoccupies you but whatever possessed anyone to

> put it on...This musical's music, by Stephen Keel
> ever, is adroit but emotionally vacuous, like the
> ings of aural wallpaper. The book by Shaun McK[illegible] and Steven Dexter is so aimlessly ridiculous, so directionless, so unwilling to exploit its comic potential that the plot's whimsy becomes an end – a very dead one – in itself." *Nicholas de Jongh, Evening Standard.*

And this, from the Financial Times:

> "It cannot be said too often that the modern musical is the cesspit of theatre today: that it is an array of synthetic emotion, synthetic characterisation, synthetic lines, synthetic melodies. The latest to hit the West End – like a soggy cosh – is *Maddie.* One blushes for Shaftesbury Avenue."

Some people who work in the theatre claim never to read reviews until after the end of the run. One director of note who claims this may not read his reviews but has his assistant give him "the gist" over coffee. Not reading reviews is probably a wise move, if one is grown up enough to manage it. The temptation, though, is almost overwhelming.

You can tell yourself that "it's only an opinion" but it is a bit like being told your child is ugly and stupid. It's hard to take it objectively. There's another dichotomy too. To believe the good things that are said, one must also believe the bad things. Besides, the praise critics give you doesn't stick in your mind. The abuse does. It can scar you for life. McKenna says to this day that he will never forget opening one newspaper to read, "McKenna's lyrics are serviceable but never once interesting." Ouch.

While it's easy to dismiss the press comment as "yesterday's chip wrapping", a well turned phrase can stick in the public's mind. "Maddie the baddie" is one such. Later in the year, at the Evening Standard awards, Ned Sherrin announced, "Many people think the award for Best Direction should go to the exit signs at *Maddie.*" I never forgave him (though he did later apologise).

Kenny Wax says:

> There's a difference between a three or four star review and the kind of five star, "selling" review that says, "This is the funniest show in the West End, you won't have a better time." It's the "selling review" that makes the difference. "Charming" is the kiss of death – you never want to see that in a review. "Hamilton" or "Book of Mormon" would never be described as charming.
>
> For the Telegraph, Charles Spencer quite correctly said he shouldn't review it again because of his part in getting it to London. Kate Basset's review was good but not the kind of "show we've been waiting for" rave that might have been that elusive "selling review."

These days social media has a huge impact, as do internet reviews by real people. All there was to go on then was "word of mouth", which depended on getting people into the show in the first place so that they could tell their friends and colleagues how much they loved it (or, for that matter, the opposite).

Kenny Wax did everything he could. Tickets went on sale at the half price booth in Leicester Square and Kenny himself went down there regularly to hand out leaflets and encourage people to give us a try. The question now was whether *Maddie* could survive.

In retrospect, Wax says:

> In all honesty - and I know this now from twenty years of experience – we had to be a quick hit. We had a

> very small advance – about £50,000, which seemed low even twenty years ago. Looking at it now, the daily wraps were so low – the "daily wraps" being what you take from all sources – that without a boost from the reviews we couldn't have gone on. With a really good set of reviews, we possibly could have gone on for a few months. On all my shows now I now get hourly wraps from 9am till midnight, so I'm totally plugged in to how a show is performing and can read the patterns. That comes with experience and I didn't have it then. Nica Burns and Richard Johnson, who ran the Lyric then for Stoll Moss, must have known that we had next to no chance without the reviews because they were used to seeing those patterns. They were immensely supportive but also immensely businesslike. Once you open, you're always balancing money. Pre-production capitalisation is gone and then you have to balance your weekly running cost with weekly takings at the box office. If you're a little bit under or over you can sometimes stagger through but it must have been obvious to Nica that we weren't going to do that for long.

The standard form of contract between a producer and theatre owner means that if a show's takings fall below the break-even point for a certain number of consecutive weeks (usually four), the theatre can give the producer two weeks notice to quit. This is known as "the notice" and it is posted backstage on the Saturday two weeks before closing night.

"Word of mouth" did have some effect. Audience numbers began to build and there was a lot of support from musical theatre fans. A lot of people said they loved the show. Unfortunately, there simply was not enough cash in the coffers to massage the box office returns (oh yes, that's standard practice) and the upturn in business would prove to be too little, too late. By the time the notice went up, the company had already read in Baz Bamigboye's *Daily Mail* showbusiness column that the RSC's production of *Cyrano de Bergerac* starring Antony Sher was heading into the Lyric for a short season.

One important thing Kenny achieved was to record the Original London Cast album. It was recorded in a single day, immediately after the show closed.

Summer Rognlie recalls:

> "*Maddie* was a project of pure love, 'The Little Engine that Could'. Truly something that will stay with me forever. Maddie is and always will be one of my greatest accomplishments and experiences of all my days in theatre."

The last, emotional performance of *Maddie*'s West End run took place on November 8th 1997, after just six weeks. A week later, Lynda Baron threw a lunch for the company at which tears were shed and laughs were had. We all left miserable, though. There's nothing quite like the feeling of emptiness when a show closes, even a successful one. When it has not been a success, after eight years of work, it takes months if not years to recover.

We did all recover, of course, and we all moved on to new projects. Dexter, Keeling and McKenna worked together again a couple of years later when Dexter directed *La Cava* at the Victoria Palace and McKenna and Keeling were brought on board to revise and expand the score and lyrics. They also wrote a musical based both on the life of Johanna Spyri, the Swiss author, and her most successful creation, *Heidi*. It was a big success in a spectacular open air production in Switzerland in 2005-6 and spawned not one but two acclaimed sequels in 2007-8. They were also commissioned by a German publishing house to write a sequel to *Peter Pan*.

Kenny Wax did not give up producing. He has gone on to a successful career with *Top Hat* winning three Laurence Olivier Awards including 'Best New Musical' from its seven nominations and his subsequent support of a group of ex drama students from LAMDA who formed The Mischief Theatre Company and with whom he has had several hugely successful West End and worldwide productions - *The Play That Goes Wrong* (Winner of the Laurence Olivier Award for Best New Comedy), *The Comedy About A Bank Robbery*, *Peter Pan Goes Wrong* (Olivier Award Nominee), *Groan Ups* and *Magic Goes Wrong*. He also produced the hit musical *Six*, about the wives of Henry VIII. In addition he has produced numerous touring shows all over the country including large scale musicals and plays and has a thriving Childrens & Family division which produces amongst other titles, *Hetty Feather* (Olivier Award Nominee), *The Gruffalo, We're Going On A Bearhunt, Room On The Broom* and *Mr Popper's Penguins*.

Steven Dexter has directed all over the world, having become something of an expert in developing and shaping new musicals. He directed the world premieres of the Olivier Award winning *Honk*, by Stiles and Drewe, at Newbury and the Olivier-nominated *Loserville* at YMT, West Yorkshire Playhouse and the Garrick Theatre. Other West End credits include *La Cava,*

Romance Romance, *Peter Pan* and *The Pirates of Penzance.* UK and European premieres include *Lucky Stiff, Altar Boyz, Saving Jason* and *The Pros the Con and a Screw.* He has had a long-standing artistic relationship with Singapore where he has created and directed *Forbidden City, Fried Rice Paradise, A Twist Of Fate, Sing To The Dawn* and *The LKY Musical,* as well as productions of *They're Playing Our Song* and *Little Shop of Horrors.* In Israel his credits include *Honk, The Full Monty, Shirley Valentine, Mary Lou, Song and Dance* and *High School Musical.* For Above The Stag in London he has directed *Romance Romance, Closer To Heaven, Beautiful Thing, Rupert Street Lonely Hearts Club, When Harry Met Barry, Fanny and Stella* and *The Sins of Jack Saul.* He has also worked extensively for British Youth Music Theatre. As well as *Maddie*, he has co-written *A Twist of Fate*, *Fagin* and *Mary Lou*.

Stephen Keeling, outside his work with Shaun McKenna, has written musicals with two award-winning authors, *Sea Change* with Michelle Magorian and *Night Shoot* with Jonathan Miles. With the late Stephen Clark he has written the music for *My Father's Son* (Crucible, Sheffield) and a one-woman musical *All The Lonely Things*. With Ed Hardy he has composed the score for a musical adaptation of *The Amazing Mr Blunden*. Stephen has also been commissioned to write the scores for several plays including *Peer Gynt* and *The Broken Heart* (Lyric Hammersmith Studio). Stephen has composed an extensive amount of choral music and has recently written a *Requiem* which was premiered in 2017.

Shaun McKenna has developed a versatile and award-winning career across theatre, radio drama and TV. His stage version of *The Lord of the Rings* (with music by A.R.Rahman, Varttina and Christopher Nightingale) ran in Toronto in 2005 and at the Theatre Royal, Drury Lane in 2006-7, winning a mantelpiece-full of awards (including a Canadian DORA for Best new Musical and an Olivier nomination). He divides his work between original work and adaptations, and has written dark thrillers for

ITV as well as contributing to long running series such as *Heartbeat.* He especially loves radio and has written a great many radio dramas for the BBC, including *Home Front* (Outstanding Achievement in Radio Award 2019), *China Towns, The Forsytes* and the *Complete Smiley* series. He has now adapted five books by leading thriller writer Peter James for the stage. In 2012 McKenna's stage version of *Ladies In Lavender* won five Broadway World awards, including Best Regional Play. With Leighton James House he wrote Terry Pratchett's *Only You Can Save Mankind,* songs for a new musical with Simon Spencer, *Are You As Nervous As I Am?* and the forthcoming *Trouser Bar.* With Chet Walker and Guy Kitchenn, he has created *Being Jack Cole.*

The three writers remain friends. After *Maddie* sank out of sight, and Warner Chappell decided not to publish the script and score, the show went into abeyance for a while. In retrospect, neither McKenna nor Dexter were entirely happy with the West End version but they never seemed to have time to sit down together and rework it.

But just as in the story, *Maddie* refuses to lie down.

In 2008, after a long conversation on Skype, a few weeks of frantic activity took place. There were two areas which McKenna had always thought problematical. One was that the show was not set at a specific date. Logically, it had to be the late 1970s, otherwise Al would have been either decrepit or dead. When the show was performed in the 1990s the 70s were too recent for the show to count as a period piece. Time having marched on, this could easily be addressed by sketching in some social background.

The second issue was Mrs van Arc who – with the writers' increasing age and maturity *[one hopes. SMcK]*- seemed to be a rather two dimensional sexually rapacious older woman. The song *Knick Knacks*, with its single extended joke, only served to emphasize this. There had to be a way of motivating Mrs van Arc's predatory behaviour while making her funnier and more lovable.

Dexter and McKenna set about writing a new version of the show. A new opening number, "Piece of Heaven" firmly rooted the story in 1977 with references to Watergate, Vietnam and the premiere of *Star Wars*. Mrs van Arc was given a motive for blackmailing Nick – Abe had left her all but bankrupt and she needed Nick to validate the one painting she had left to her name. Unfortunately, the said painting was a fake. In cahoots with a new character – a bewigged lawyer named Morton, who has adored her for years – Mrs van Arc reluctantly set about inveigling Nick into a honey trap.

These two developments were great – but unfortunately McKenna and Dexter didn't stop there. They ended up scissor happy and threw out far too many of the existing songs, persuading Keeling to write half a dozen new (less successful) numbers to replace them. In short, the baby was thrown out with the bathwater. The reception, when they showed the result to Kenny Wax and McKenna's agent, was appalled disbelief – and once again *Maddie* went back into the bottom drawer.

Which is where it stayed until the spring of 2016 when the enterprising Tim Hutton of Stage Door Records had the idea to reissue the Original Cast Album CD.

Hutton recalls:

> I first contacted Stephen Keeling and Shaun McKenna in Spring 2015 when we were compiling material for the Stage Door album *Lost West End.* The premise of the album was to showcase one "lift out" song from 20 unique forgotten West End musicals of the late 20th century. The aim was to give listeners an opportunity to rediscover the musicals featured while

at the same time introducing those shows (and their scores) to a new audience. Two of the musicals we especially wanted to feature were *Maddie* and *La Cava* and we were thrilled when both McKenna and Keeling were happy to be involved and contribute a song from each musical to the project.

Lost West End was released in July 2015 and both the public and critics' reaction took us by complete surprise. The CD was highlighted as an "Essential New Release" in The Sunday Times and the album was serialised in a month long feature on Elaine Paige's BBC Radio 2 programme. The first track to be played by Paige was the *Maddie* duet *Don't Look Back* and the response was fantastic. In fact many felt it was the highlight and "go to" track on the album.

The reaction to *Don't Look Back* made a big impression. I'd always thoroughly enjoyed the *Maddie* Original London Cast Album; the music was stunning and incredibly immediate while the lyrics were both witty and moving. We're always eager to explore ideas for future cast album releases and the prospect of reissuing the *Maddie* London Cast Album seemed particularly pertinent as the original CD was now long out of print and fast becoming a collector's item in its own right.

In January 2016 Stephen Keeling uploaded to his Soundcloud channel a piano / vocal demo of the *Maddie* song *Star* performed by Jacqui Scott. After sampling the track, I enquired with Stephen how many demos were recorded during the show's development and what artists were involved on those recordings. To my astonishment, Stephen reeled off a literal "Who's Who" list of West End stars; John Barrowman,

Mary Millar, Helen Hobson, Greg Ellis, Lorna Dallas, to name but a few. With such an abundance of material, the notion of reissuing *Maddie* as an Expanded Deluxe Edition Cast Album seemed perfect, particularly with the added bonus of including several cut numbers from the score and alternate versions of the existing songs.

As Stage Door is a label that specialise in preserving 'lost' West End theatre scores, we would normally issue a cast album as a stand alone recording. The proposed *Maddie* concept offered something that was unique and to my knowledge a first, no cast recording to date had been reissued with such a wealth of bonus material and in effect would give musical theatre fans the opportunity to chart the show's development from page to stage.

A meeting was organised with Stephen and Shaun at the National Theatre in February 2016 to discuss the reissue in more detail. There was a great vibe and rapport at that meeting which continued throughout the whole process of working together on the album. It was agreed that the CD should be issued in September / October 2016 to coincide with the 20th anniversary of *Maddie* opening in Salisbury. Stephen had managed to locate all the tapes from the various demo sessions recorded between 1990-1997 and after transferring the material to digital format, what stood out was the quality of both the material and the recordings. We were spoiled for choice as to what material to include and the prospect of featuring such a wealth of unreleased material performed by so many leading West End performers was extremely exciting.

> As the project developed, what became apparent when compiling the running order with Stephen and Shaun for the "Bonus Disc" was that the bulk of the featured material was drawn from two recording sessions held at London's Air-Edel Studios in November 1991 and November 1992. Although Stephen had found excellent condition cassette tapes of these recordings, where possible we always like to work from the source master tapes for an album release. At an extreme long shot, we contacted Air-Edel Studios to enquire whether they had kept the original DAT masters for the two *Time Of My Life* sessions. Taking into consideration the likelihood of Air-Edel keeping DAT tapes from 25 years earlier was less than slim, it was with sheer amazement when an email came through two weeks later from Tom Bullen, the studio manager at Air-Edel, to say we were in luck, they had found the masters! Suddenly hearing all these incredible recordings from the master tape was like hearing the material in full colour where all the intricacies and nuances of the performances could be fully appreciated.

Tim Hutton's interest sparked an idea. With the new generation of producers, and a new generation of off West End venues devoted to musicals, might it be time for *Maddie* to re-emerge? It was certainly worth looking at.

Once the writers re-engaged with the material, it was a relatively straightforward matter for McKenna and Dexter to create a "definitive" new version of the show. They combined the few but vivid virtues of the 2009 rewrite with everything that was great about the West End version. Songs that had been cut or changed as long ago as Oxford were re-examined and one or two of them were reinstated in the show, with adjusted lyrics. By the time the marketing for the Twentieth Anniversary De Luxe CD was under way, the writers had created a mid-sized musical, with some ensemble numbers, which could be offered to those new London venues. It was retitled *Maddie And Me,* to help make people think of it as a new show, not a revival of something that had failed long ago. This was particularly important for the American market, of which there was some hopes.

Maddie and Me contained three songs – two new, one from the very first draft - which had either never been recorded or existed only in a very poor copy. It was decided to record new piano demos of them. Keeling contacted Goldsmith's College, where he had studied, as they have an excellent small recording studio with brilliant technicians.

Tim Hutton recalls:

> While work on finalising the tracklisting for the Bonus Disc continued, Stephen emailed various home demos of the 2008 rewrite which included a beautiful new song called *There We Were*. Stephen said at some point he would like to have the number recorded with a musical theatre performer and I immediately suggested it would be a perfect song for Meredith Braun. Meredith originated the role of Betty Schaeffer in Andrew Lloyd Webber's *Sunset Boulevard* and also starred as Eponine in *Les Miserables* and Christine in *The Phantom Of The Opera.* Meredith had recorded her debut solo album for Stage Door five years earlier and we'd both very much wanted to work together again on a new project. It emerged that Stephen had in fact met Meredith years before when working on his musical *My Father's Son* in Sheffield and agreed Meredith would be the perfect vocalist for the track.
>
> The session proved a triumph, not just for Meredith's terrific vocal on *There We Were* but also for the excel-

lent recording of *Feeling This Way with You*, one of the first songs written for *Maddie* which was performed superbly by Dominic Hodson. Such was the success of the two new recordings that a further session was organised in July to record another of the new *Maddie* songs; the charismatic duet *Maybe We Should Marry*, performed terrifically by Moir Leslie and Alister Cameron. The addition of the 3 new 2016 recordings on the *Maddie* Deluxe Album gave the release an extra polish and brought the journey of the musical full circle.

The Album was released on October 14th and was very well received. It received a lot of airplay on specialist radio programmes and attracted some very good reviews. It was an innovation to utilize so much additional material – since then, many other cast albums have followed suit.

> “This 2-CD set includes some truly hummable songs from the original cast recording that I haven't been able to get out of my head since re-acquainting myself with Stephen Keeling's music and Shaun McKenna's lyrics.” *Mark Smith, musicast.co.uk*

> “The score deftly blends period sounds and contemporary ones, perfect for a tale of characters from two very different time periods.” *Bwaytunes.com*

> “It's songs, I think, rank up there with anything you can compare it to... Great orchestrations by Caroline Humphris... But what I'm most impressed about on this issue are the three 2016 tracks and of course the demos – the real value and interest for any collector like me. They are worth the price and effort of the release alone. The three 2016 tracks are just wonderful – a perfect blend of great material and superb performances. The standout track here, and probably on the album, is Meredith Braun's recording of *There We Were*, but to be honest all three tracks have merit... It was also great to hear John Barr and Jacqui Scott again – in my mind, two of the most unerrated theatre actors in the UK.” *Ian Gude, reviewgraveyard.com*

> “A cracking collection of songs that are sure to hit the right notes with musical theatre buffs and inspire budding composers with a rarely heard collection of well-constructed and performed songs.” *Greg James, Entertainment Focus*

As the album came out, almost twenty years to the day after that first performance in Salisbury, we planned to issue this book. Though it had been conceived originally as a marketing tool for what we presumed would be our first mega-hit show, it now seemed like an interesting record of a period – the sort of thing which would be of interest to musical theatre buffs.

Then there was a development – and it looked as though *Maddie And Me* might be heading for a new life and a new production in the USA.

In 2015, Shaun started working closely with American choreographer and director, Chet Walker. They shared a New York agent at the time who put them together to discuss a potential reworking of the forgotten 1950s hit show, *Irma La Douce*. That project foundered but Chet brought Shaun onto a much more exciting project, *Feelin' In The Mood*. This was a show about Glenn Miller and his wife, to be produced by American producer in London Kim Poster. Chet and Shaun found themselves so *simpatico* and creatively in tune that between them they started to develop a whole raft of new shows. One is the forthcoming musical *Being Jack Cole* about the genius who invented jazz dance long before Fosse, Agnes deMille and Jerome Robbins came on the scene.

Chet loved *Maddie and Me* and sent it to some friends, who responded equally positively. When Shaun was in New York in the summer of 2018, to work with Chet and Stephen Schwartz on a ballet based on Schwartz's song *Boy On The Roof* at the Jacob's Pillow Festival, Chet set up a meeting with designer David Sumner and the doyen of special effects, Richard Gonci. Gonci had come up with an idea for a revolutionary way to put a ghost on stage – a three-dimensional ghost who would look solid to the audience but whom an actor could walk through, if need be. It promised to be expensive but revolutionary technology for those moments when Maddie possesses Jan and Mrs van Arc, finally leaving at the end to dissolve back into the universe. There was much excitement and the four men formed a company to explore this further.

At the same time, Chet and Shaun were talking to producer Curtis Howard about a smaller-scale New York version of the show – hoping the two strands could be brought together. Howard is a dynamic young producer with a very astute eye. On reading the latest draft, he had some issues.

The #MeToo movement had taken the world by storm. Harvey Weinstein was accused of rape and all over the world women (and men) were coming forward with horrible accounts of unwanted sexual attentions that had been forced on them. Kevin Spacey and Bill Cosby were the most high-profile of a slew of performers whose careers foundered. The #MeToo movement led to a worldwide reassessment of the ideas of consent and power within sexual relationships. It became harder – and perceived as inauthentic – for men to write about women. Shaun had already found this in his work at the BBC – he was no longer being considered to adapt books by women writers.

Curtis Howard felt that, because of when *Maddie And Me* was written, there were certain inherent assumptions about the characters and their situations which were reflective of the attitudes of the 1990s rather than now - or of the 1970s when it was set. He felt especially for Jan – as if she was being blamed for not being as exciting and adventurous as Maddie. He asked Shaun to re-examine the script to ensure that all the women were three dimensional and their attitudes, positions and dignity were all respected.

Approaching a script you have rewritten a hundred times from a new perspective is incredibly unsettling – but it ultimately proved to be incredibly rewarding. The changes were small but some of the knock-on effects proved very significant. Working with Dexter and Keeling, in April 2019 Shaun produced a revised script which retains all the mad romantic farce which made the original so appealing – but, significantly, also creates strong, independent women who do not in any way need a man to fulfil or validate them. It is, without question, the best version to date – not least, perhaps, because all the creators have grown older and wiser in the intervening period.

Shows, as we have seen, take time to come together. Since April 2019, progress has slowed but not halted. All the creative team members have been occupied with other projects, love affairs, illnesses, babies, family dramas and all the other aspects of daily life which can delay a creative process. Now comes COVID-19 which has thrown the whole house of cards up into the air – nobody knows which projects will survive or when theatres will open their doors again.

One thing is certain, however. Maddie won't lie down – and *Maddie And Me* will see the light of day once more. As recently as last week (at the time of writing) a young producer asked for all the available material.

She'll be back. It's only a matter of time. As Maddie herself would say:

Last time it was snatched away,
This time, gonna have my day.
There's no sense in thinking small.
Now it's my turn, I'm gonna have it all.

Watch this space.

RESOURCES

Maddie – Original Cast recording - the DeLuxe 2CD 20th Anniversary Edition is available from Stage Door Records - http://www.stagedoorrecords.com/stage9047.html
It can also be downloaded on iTunes.

Musical Scores
Sheet music for many of the songs from *Maddie* can be downloaded at
https://www.scoreexchange.com/profiles/stephenkeeling

Videos
A number of videos of songs from *Maddie*, with subtitles, are available on the YouTube channel McKennaKeeling.
https://www.youtube.com/user/McKennaKeeling

Sound Recordings

The complete recording of *In Company With Sondheim* is available on Stephen Keeling's Soundcloud channel.
https://soundcloud.com/stephen-keeling-1/in-company-with-sondheim-maddie

Sound recordings from *Maddie* and other shows by Stephen Keeling are available on
https://soundcloud.com/stephen-keeling-1

Websites

Stephen Keeling: http://www.stephenkeeling.org.uk
Shaun McKenna: https://www.shaunmckenna.me
Kenny Wax: https://kennywax.com
Caroline Humphris:https://www.carolinehumphris.com
